CHRISTIAN FAITH SERIES

CONSULTING EDITOR: *Reinhold Niebuhr*

Hardness of Heart

HARDNESS
OF
HEART

A Contemporary

Interpretation

of the Doctrine

of Sin

by E. La B. Cherbonnier

———————————————

1955

DOUBLEDAY & COMPANY, INC.

Garden City, New York

Library of Congress Catalog Card Number 55-5500

TO A. L. C. AND E. G. C.

PREFACE

This book attempts to correlate the biblical understanding of sin with the facts of modern life. It will argue that the Bible, far from being irrelevant to the twentieth century, is in fact indispensable to it, that the problems of our day raise questions to which only the biblical religion has ever claimed to have an answer.

The implication is that the Bible will yield a philosophy of life which can sustain itself on independent grounds. It is often maintained, to the contrary, that many different philosophies appear in the Bible and that to select one of them and label it "biblical" is arbitrary. Actually, however, recent scholarship has disclosed a far greater unity in the Bible than was formerly supposed. The method underlying the present essay has been to ask: What unspoken philosophical assumptions does the Bible make when it is not talking philosophy at all—that is, about ninety-nine per cent of the time? When the answers to this question are correlated, they comprise a remarkably consistent world view, spanning over ten centuries and including scores of writers. It is this over-all unity of philosophical outlook which will be designated herein as "biblical."

The residue of inconsistencies which admittedly exists thus ceases to be a problem. The Bible provides its own internal principle of self-criticism, by which these odds and ends can legitimately be identified as falling outside the overwhelming import of the Bible as a whole. The following pages attempt to reduce some of this biblical wisdom to the language of reasoned argument.

I should like to express my gratitude to all who have contributed directly or indirectly to the book. I am especially indebted to Reinhold Niebuhr, not only for a critical reading of the text and for valuable suggestions which have spared me many an infelicity, but also for a dozen years of counsel and stimulus. Although not liable for the book's conclusions, his influence is evident throughout.

Finally, Mr. and Mrs. Robert D. Newton, together with Spessard Caldwell, have spent more time and effort in improving the text than I could possibly repay.

E. La B. C.

Barnard College
April, 1955

CONTENTS

Hardness of Heart

HUMANISM VERSUS ORTHODOXY

God is not the author of confusion, but of peace.
—1 Corinthians 14:33

If there is any viable alternative to it, the Christian doctrine of sin ought not to be taken seriously. Its consequences are far too momentous to warrant acceptance on any but the most unimpeachable grounds. The most obvious alternative is to deny that the conception of sin in any form, whether Christian or otherwise, is a meaningful or necessary category for the interpretation of human life. As against this view, the present book must demonstrate that some notion of sin, even though under a different label, is integral to the thinking of every human being. He who denies it ultimately succeeds only in concealing it from himself.

The other alternative to the Christian view would indeed retain the conception of sin but with a different definition. Historically all such definitions have fallen under one of two main headings: the moralistic view, which regards sin as the violation of given rules and standards; and the dismal conception of sin as some intrinsic defect in human nature. The book must therefore also refute these versions of sin before vindicating the specifically biblical view.

According to the Bible, sin is properly defined as misplaced allegiance or, to use its technical word for it, idolatry. No man is without his "god," in the sense of a focal point around which his life takes its orbit and which imparts a distinctive complexion to his values, purposes, and actions. The task of substantiating this conception has been complicated by the failure of Christian orthodoxy always to distinguish it clearly from the other two. Christian thinking has tended historically to assimilate one or the other of them, particularly the notion of sin as intrinsic to human nature. In the popular mind this is precisely what the phrase "original sin" connotes. This puts the theologian in the unenviable position of endorsing a view which the Bible itself repudiates. Its pagan origin, as well as the disparagement of human existence which follows from it, is recalled in the following anecdote from Friedrich Nietzsche:

There is an ancient story that King Midas hunted in the forest a long time for the wise Silenus, the companion of Dionysus, without capturing him. When Silenus at last fell into his hands, the king asked what was the best and most desirable of all things for man. Fixed and immovable, the demigod said not a word; till at last, urged by the king, he gave a shrill laugh and broke into these words: "Oh, wretched ephemeral race, children of chance and misery, why do ye compel me to tell you what it were most expedient for you not to hear? What is best of all is beyond your reach forever: not to be born, not to *be*, to be *nothing*. But the second best for you is—quickly to die."[1]

The pagan world has no real defense against this sophisticated infection. When serious thinkers outside the Judaeo-Christian tradition have squarely faced the problem, they have to an alarming extent succumbed to it.

The awkwardness of the extreme orthodox position is nicely illustrated by its current disadvantage in discussions with thoughtful non-Christians, especially those of a broad humanitarian concern. Having absorbed indirectly the genuine biblical emphasis upon the dignity and worth of man, modern humanists are now obliged to repudiate Christianity in order to defend these principles! When men like John Dewey, Horace Kallen, and Erich Fromm accuse Christianity of devaluating worldly existence and the good things of life, one is embarrassed by how many theological citations they can muster in support of the charge. Little suspecting that the foundation for their own ideals is to be found in the Bible, they abhor the doctrine of sin as an affront to the dignity and creativity of man, a medieval superstition invented by the priesthood to block progress and keep the ignorant in subjection to sacerdotal privilege.

Hence the humanist rejoices that the advance of science has not only helped to overthrow an oppressive institution but also defied the pessimistic teachings which he attributes to Christianity. In so far as he opposes the devaluation of earthly existence he is in fact the unwitting champion of the biblical view as against theological distortions of it. An outstanding example is Lionel Trilling, who writes:

And if we are ill we are ill . . . not by a universal necessity, (but) by a fault in the economy of our powers, not by the nature of the powers themselves.[2]

[1]Friedrich Nietzsche, "The Birth of Tragedy," in *The Philosophy of Nietzsche* (New York: Random House, The Modern Library, n.d.), pp. 961f.
[2]Lionel Trilling, "Art and Neurosis," in *The Liberal Imagination* (New York: Doubleday Anchor Books, 1953), p. 177. Professor Trilling attributes the illness of man to a universal accident, an illuminating humanistic alternative to the biblical conception of responsibility.

If the tide of argument appears to be running with the humanist, however, his advantage is only temporary. When obliged to defend his position, he encounters formidable difficulties of his own. It is one thing simply to assert the dignity of man but quite another to establish it by argument. His case collapses the moment he is pressed for a rationale. This becomes evident when he confronts the catalogue of atrocities in the past and the present history of the race—that is, when the *fact* of sin stares him squarely in the face. Fearing that to admit the reality of sin would impugn the dignity of man, he searches for an alternative interpretation of the grim realities. His only recourse is to deny on principle that man is even *capable* of sin. But this expedient, by robbing man of his freedom, has the opposite of its intended effect. Instead of preserving human nobility it forfeits it. For, although to commit sin is certainly no compliment, the ability to do so *is*. Only if man *can* do evil is there any meaning in doing good. Only if he is free can creative action be distinguished from destructive.

A perfect illustration of the humanist's dilemma is provided by Erich Fromm's recent book, *Man for Himself*, whose explicit purpose is to construct a humanistic ethic. The author begins with a glorification of human freedom and the creative capacities of man. By the end of the book, however, he has provided so much clinical evidence for the fact of sin that he reverses himself and adopts a deterministic view.[3]

His reluctance to recognize the full implications of the human freedom which he sometimes exalts leads the humanist to contract an injudicious alliance. Having hailed science as the liberator of mankind, he credulously embraces a philosophy which purports to be based upon it: not simply science as a method, but the dogma that there is no other method. From the standpoint of this dogma human freedom is neither possible nor desirable. It is not possible, because of the assumption that human behavior can be exhaustively explained in causal terms. It is not desirable because it would introduce an element of incalculability into the scientist's field of study. Man is reduced either to the status of a cog in a machine, whose only distinguishing characteristic is a certain cog-consciousness; or he is submerged in an undertow of biological impulses which make a mockery of his fancied rational intentions. In either case the de-

[3]Erich Fromm, *Man for Himself* (New York: Rinehart & Co., Inc., 1947). Compare Chapter 1 with Chapter 4, subdivision 5.

personalization of man is accomplished. Why not put him in a concentration camp and make him, like any other guinea pig, the subject of macabre experiments?

The intellectual impotence of humanism to answer this question
has been so thoroughly exposed by authors like Reinhold Niebuhr
that it hardly seems sporting to rub it in any further. Suffice it to
mention a recent book, not from the pen of a theologian at all, but
of one of the wisest of contemporary humanists, Joseph Wood
Krutch. In his *The Measure of Man* he analyzes some startling por-
tents in the recent utterances of "scientific humanists." He concludes:

How defective, therefore, is that so-called Science of Man which never
really asks the questions at all and thus proves itself to be, not the Science
of Man, but only the Science-Of-What-Man-Would-Be-If-He-Were-Not-
A-Man-But-A-Machine . . . While we have exalted man's importance by
making his "welfare" the measure of all things, we have, at the same time,
belittled him by assuming that he is, nevertheless, nothing in himself.
. . . The grand paradox of our society is this: we magnify man's rights
but we minimize his capacities. And it is only in some totalitarian theory
that this paradox can be resolved. Sub-men cannot rule themselves.[4]

The humanist case against orthodoxy thus backfires. Having
charged his opponent with disparaging the greatness and goodness of
man, he finds that he lives in a glass house. The orthodox theologian
replies, in effect, "We merely develop with greater consistency the
same principles which you yourself acknowledge." The situation acquires a touch of irony from the fact that, although the theologian
wins the argument, the humanist's lost cause is nevertheless one
which the Christian not only ought to defend but is also in the best
position to substantiate. For the goodness of created existence, the
worth and meaningfulness of human life, if not the monopoly of the
Bible, at least find their strongest support there. Current discussion
sometimes offers the spectacle of the theologian, under the exigencies
of debate with the humanist, resorting to a denial of the worth and
value of human existence, reveling in anxiety as a virtue, and preach-
ing despair as the Christian gospel.

In a day when the world is more ready than at any time since the
early centuries to hear the good news of Christianity, contemporary
theology is in danger of succumbing to the *mal du siècle* and handing
the world a stone. Small wonder that men like Joseph Wood Krutch,
Lionel Trilling, and Jacques Barzun, though they have seen the fatal

[4]Joseph Wood Krutch, *The Measure of Man* (New York: The Bobbs-Merrill
Company, Inc., 1954), pp. 169f., 200f.

weakness of the humanist position, still cling forlornly to it as at least preferable to what they expect to hear in the name of theology. They are at a loss to understand how intelligent, public-spirited Christians can associate themselves with what to them is a defeatist and obscurantist position.

When partisans to the two sides of debate must vindicate themselves by pointing to the other's weakness, then the argument has somewhere taken a wrong turn. It is time to begin again and inquire what false premise has insinuated itself into the thinking of both sides. If such a premise can be detected and replaced, then there is hope of a fresh start, a genuine third alternative which can combine the strength and avoid the pitfalls of the rival factions.

As the foregoing discussion suggests, the error common to both orthodoxy and humanism is the failure consistently to appreciate the fact of human freedom. While the one disregards it in the name of science, the other accomplishes a similar effect by defining sin as a constitutional necessity of human nature, outside the realm of responsibility and freedom.

By contrast, the biblical version of sin as idolatry, or misplaced allegiance, is based squarely upon the fact of freedom. Indeed, it follows from it so inevitably that no one who grants the latter can consistently deny the former. The book's first step, in Part I, is therefore to persuade both humanist and orthodox theologian that human freedom cannot logically be denied. Once this is granted, the definition of sin as idolatry follows automatically. Part II will show how an insufficient appreciation of human freedom has induced Christian thinking to exchange the biblical understanding of sin for an indiscriminate disparagement of human nature. Part III will validate the conception of idolatry in both theory and practice. The implication for Christian thought is that there is a biblical wisdom which constitutes its strongest weapon; for the humanist, that the authentic doctrine of sin, far from being opposed to a true humanism, is in fact indispensable to it.

Part I
Man, the Religious Animal

in which it is argued that, consciously or otherwise, everyone has a definition of sin, and that the proper question is not *whether* to use the word but, rather, *which* conception of sin is correct.

CHAPTER II

GOOD AND EVIL: EVERYBODY'S PROBLEM

> Woe to them that call good evil and evil good.
> —Isaiah 5:20

Anyone who uses the word "sin" obviously assumes a distinction between good and evil. But this distinction has frequently been challenged by leaders of thought, both scientific and philosophic. A discussion of sin must therefore first deal with the question of whether, in the last analysis, the difference between good and evil is tenable or whether it is merely a subjective phenomenon which a man of intelligence can overcome. If it can be successfully suppressed, then all talk about sin becomes a dead issue. But if not, then sin at once becomes everybody's problem.

He who wishes to avoid this problem correctly concentrates his fire upon value judgments. His campaign acquires momentum from the fact that they have so often been harmfully applied in an area where they do not belong. They have been used, whether by infallible Church or by infallible Party, to dictate the results of inquiries which ought properly to be answered in terms of true or false, not good or bad. Rightly rejecting such "ideology," some philosophers and scientists have taken the further step by trying to eliminate value judgments altogether, or at least to banish them to a subrational compartment of the personality, in the hope of reducing them eventually to the vanishing point.

The present chapter, by illustrating the failure of these attempts, will suggest that they are in principle impossible. No one can censor the word "good" and "evil" without introducing some substitute for them, and no one can put them in quarantine without presupposing them. Even the legitimate suspension of value judgments for purposes of scientific investigation occurs within a total context of valuation. The scientist must first decide that it is "good" to seek objective truth. To make the further decision that it would be even "better" to dispense completely with the terms "good" and "evil" would repudiate the basis of the decision itself. It is therefore not surprising that everyone who attempts to banish these terms becomes the victim of a curious irony. The harder he tries to exclude them from life as a whole, the more they intrude into the subordinate areas where they are inappropriate. This is the first illustration of a principle which will recur throughout the book: No false premise can be consistently elaborated; this is the last laugh which the truth enjoys at the expense of all misconceptions of it. The following pages will apply this principle to some significant attempts to extinguish or compartmentalize value judgments.

The standard argument against them is that they are merely relative, that they reflect only the private preferences of the individual. Words denoting value, such as "good" and "right," are all reducible to terms of taste, either personal or social. From Protagoras to Bertrand Russell, the relativist's favorite argument is based upon the lack of unanimity concerning the standard by which good and evil are judged. The conception of precisely what is good varies from culture to culture and even from man to man. Among certain Eskimos, for example, it is the duty of a son to kill his father when the latter has grown too old to fend for himself. And among many primitive peoples the first duty of a good host is to lend his wife to an overnight guest. The relativist defies his opponent to prove that any of these "local customs" is "better" than another. In the absence of proof he concludes that judgments of right and wrong merely reflect private preferences.

This conclusion, however, does not follow. If people make different estimates of the temperature of a room, it by no means follows that none of their guesses is correct. If, in the days before Columbus, people disagreed as to the shape of the earth, it did not follow that none of their opinions was right. In short, lack of unanimity has nothing to do with the case.

Failing to establish his point directly, the relativist attempts an indirect proof. He says, in effect, "Let us act on the assumption that value judgments are relative. Let us see what happens if we refuse to make them. If this experiment is successful, we may safely conclude that the distinction between good and evil is a thing of the past." This proposal is entirely legitimate, but unfortunately it backfires. What it finally proves is that ethical questions possess a peculiar characteristic not shared by other problems. Where discussion about temperature or about the shape of the earth before 1492 could, by common agreement, be suspended, value judgments refuse to stay shelved. Rather, they are the precondition of every human enterprise. The relativist's experiment is itself conducted upon the assumption that to suspend moral judgments would be "good" and to make them "bad."

The following examples illustrate how every attempt to banish value judgments from intelligent life as a whole, as distinct from their deliberate suspension for special purposes, ends in self-contradiction. They all turn out to be devious ways of declaring that to distinguish good from evil is itself evil. This fact discloses something important about the nature of man. It means that man is that creature who is constitutionally obliged to make value judgments, including the judgment that they "should" be suspended in certain cases. The person who tries the hardest to eliminate them from his life as a whole turns out to be a crusader in disguise. He is sometimes the more bigoted for imagining himself to be neutral. The problem of good and evil must therefore be transposed from the question, *whether* to make the distinction, to the question, *when* to make it. And this forces the inquiry, "What is the true good?"

FUTILE ATTEMPTS TO AVOID VALUE JUDGMENTS

Of all the historic efforts to suppress value judgments, nobody insisted more strongly than Friedrich Nietzsche that moral norms are purely arbitrary. Nobody strove more manfully than he to demolish all rules of conduct on the ground that they might infringe upon the spontaneous impulse of the individual. Hence the title of his book, *Beyond Good and Evil*. The irony of his position, however, consists in his denunciation of value judgments, together with those who make them, as themselves *wicked!* The futility of his effort to get "beyond good and evil" is perfectly symbolized by the subtitle of his last book, "A Trans-valuation of All Values," in which he declared that "fair is foul, and foul is fair." That is, he simply labeled the accepted morality of his day "bad" and its opposite "good." His grandiose ambition thus came to an end with the mere substitution of one set of values for another.

Another determined attempt to deny any objective distinction between good and evil was made by the nineteenth-century philosopher, Max Stirner. He thought he could avoid the kind of embarrassment which overtook Nietzsche by sticking to the formula, "My will be done." The point at issue, of course, is not whether one can simply utter the sentence, "My will be done." Obviously it is possible to make any statement whatever. Intelligent discussion begins only when both parties acknowledge a test by which their respective contentions may be judged legitimate. "The common man," both Socrates and Protagoras agreed, "will say anything." Rational discourse, however, tests whether a statement can be maintained *consistently* or whether it betrays its author into self-contradiction.

Stirner's formula fails to pass the test. He could have made himself unassailable by simply saying, "I do what I want—period." Although such a statement is irrefutable, it is of doubtful significance. In order to communicate something of philosophic import he was obliged to maintain further that the maxim, "My will be done," is *right*. And this is his undoing. If it is right, then those who follow it exemplify "good" conduct, while those who do not are "bad." And this, of course, is precisely the implication which Stirner had set out to avoid. He too, by his resolute attempt to suppress value judgments, beautifully illustrates their inevitability.

At the present time the argument against the objective validity of value judgments is carried on by certain representatives of the sciences. Bertrand Russell puts it in a nutshell:

The chief ground for adopting this view [the relativity of value judgments] is the complete impossibility of finding any arguments to prove that this or that has intrinsic value. Since no way can even be imagined for deciding a difference as to values, the conclusion is forced upon us that the difference is one of tastes, not one as to any objective truths.[1]

The contention is that all ethical norms are relative to a given culture. This position collapses the moment one recalls that within any given culture there is always at least a leaven of dissenting and prophetic spirits who criticize the foundations of its ethical standards. Chief among them are often the social scientists themselves. Ruth Benedict, for example, in her renowned book, *Patterns of Culture*, after stubbornly refusing, in the name of science, to make any value judgment on the foreign cultures which she studies, concludes with some trenchant and far-reaching judgments upon her own! Social scientists, in fact, continually suggest ways, often very constructive ones, in which society might be changed for the better. The theory that value judgments are all culturally derived is manifestly unable to account for the creative souls who would rather drink hemlock than compromise their standards. There is no more appropriate illustration than Bertrand Russell himself. In his book *Religion and*

[1]Bertrand Russell, *Religion and Science* (Oxford University Press, 1935), p. 238.

Science his repudiation of value judgments is sandwiched between confident moral indignation against wife-burning in India, stock-broking in America, the brutality of Hitler's Germany, and censor-ship of the press and vindictive punishment everywhere. He reserves his strongest strictures for religionists and all others who commit the unpardonable sin of making value judgments. Russell has hardly finished baiting his trap before he falls into it himself.

The most piquant example of the same phenomenon occurs in George A. Lundberg's book, *Can Science Save Us?* In sublime un-awareness of the self-contradiction into which he falls the author makes the following declaration:

First of all, the advancement of the social sciences would probably deprive us in a large measure of the luxury of indignation in which we now in-dulge ourselves as regards social events. This country, for example, has recently enjoyed a great emotional vapor-bath directed at certain Euro-pean movements and leaders. Such indignation ministers to deep-seated, jungle-fed sentiment of justice, virtue, and a general feeling of the fitness of things, as compared with what a scientific diagnosis of the situation evokes. . . . Social sciences worthy of the name will have to examine realistically all the pious shibboleths which are . . . frequently the last refuge of scoundrels and bigots.[2]

Anyone who makes a value judgment is a scoundrel and a bigot! When uttered from the vaudeville stage, instead of from the pedestal of science, this kind of reasoning is readily identified as humorous. It belongs in the same category as the line about the man who said that anyone who went to a psychiatrist ought to have his head ex-amined.

In their determination to maintain a fixed neutrality some scien-tists replace the words "good" and "bad," "right" and "wrong," which would do full justice to their real problem, with various sub-stitutes, such as "mature," "adjusted," "normal," "fruitful," and even, by an incongruous turn of the wheel, the word "scientific" itself. All these words are ambiguous. In common usage they are merely de-scriptive, referring to a situation of fact: "This apple tree is more fruitful than that"; "the car's brakes are well-adjusted," and so forth. But they can also be used in a *prescriptive* way, so as subtly to com-mend one way of behavior as preferable to another. Properly speak-ing, the word "mature," for example, refers to a physiological state. It would apply equally to human beings of identical age and physical

[2]George A. Lundberg, *Can Science Save Us?* (New York: Longmans, Green, & Co., 1947), pp. 43–45.

development. But it can also convey a valuational sense. This occurs if the scientist gives his endorsement to the *behavior* of one of the two individuals by labeling it more "mature." All such words can be used with an aura of "scientific objectivity" while actually concealing a judgment of value. The unwary reader can easily become the victim of an unintended propaganda whose effectiveness is all the greater for being clothed with the authoritative mantle of science.

Nor is the reader the only victim of this verbal ambiguity. The scientist himself often reacts with genuine horror at the suggestion that he has given anything but a descriptive account of the facts. The most notable current examples are the Kinsey reports. They purport to do no more than describe human behavior, and exhibit a condescending attitude toward those who have not yet outgrown the tendency to distinguish good from evil. In actual fact, however, they adopt an unmistakable advocacy of certain kinds of behavior as opposed to others. This is most transparent in the terms which Dr. Kinsey uses to describe individuals who have "high frequencies of sexual outlet." He calls them "sexually more capable," "excellent responders," "uninhibited," "high-rating individuals." Speaking of promiscuous behavior, he says it is "biologically natural and basic." Most flagrant of all is his suggestion that sexual promiscuity correlates closely with certain traits of character which he can be fairly sure will be regarded publicly as desirable, such as energy, alertness, vivacity, spontaneity, aggressiveness, and social poise. Having made this observation, the author then grants somewhat belatedly that it was based on insufficient data and actually holds true for only fifty-three per cent of his "high-frequency" individuals.[3]

Dr. Kinsey himself steadfastly refuses to see that these passages constitute an endorsement of sexual promiscuity. He takes refuge in the claim that his intentions were purely descriptive. The point at issue, however, is not all what his motives might have been but what the implications of the book are. His refusal to accept responsibility for them is a measure of the tenacity with which the scientist clings to the illusion that value judgments can be avoided. It also illustrates the potential danger to society of the man whose left hand does not know what his right is doing.

[3]Alfred C. Kinsey, Wardell B. Pomeroy, and Clyde E. Martin, *Sexual Behavior in the Human Male* (Philadelphia: W. B. Saunders Company, 1948), pp. 325f., 542f., 574, 580.

THE INESCAPABILITY OF VALUE JUDGMENTS

The campaign against value judgments thus turns out to be itself based upon a value judgment. He who would dispense with them has already decided that they are "bad." He differs from other moralists solely in not knowing that he is one. He who argues that all value judgments are simply the product of cultural conditioning is put to silence by the simple question: What if the culture decides to require the results of scientific experiment to conform to the expediency of a party line? Clearly there can be no science at all except on the basis of a prior agreement concerning how men *ought* to behave. Confronted by this challenge to his ideal of complete neutrality, the scientist occasionally does an abrupt *volte-face* and becomes a moralist with a vengeance. Is it reasonable, he asks, for the scientist, as the most reasonable of men, to submit to an irrational system of values? The question is only rhetorical. The culture exists to make the world safe for science and must accept from qualified experts the values suitable to this purpose. Joseph Wood Krutch's *The Measure of Man* is an exquisite analysis of the spectacle of science, which has so often been the staunchest defender of the right of dissent, now making suspiciously authoritarian noises.

Closer scrutiny of this phenomenon is reserved for a later chapter. The one remaining question for present purposes is: Are the foregoing illustrations simply cases in which the particular scientist or philosopher failed to practice what he preached? Might a more determined effort succeed where he failed? The argument has been that the decision to suspend value judgments, even for the legitimate purposes of abstract knowledge, itself rests upon a value judgment. The contradictions which overtake such attempts represent, not accidental oversights, but the nemesis which awaits all who tacitly presuppose what they explicitly deny.

The conclusion is that to distinguish between good and evil is a built-in necessity for every man. To be sure, a number of difficult problems would be eliminated at a stroke if one could banish these words. Bertrand Russell's reason for trying to do so is quite frankly to avoid the perplexing problem which otherwise arises, that of determining which is *the* good. The effort to reduce complex questions to simple terms is of course fundamental to scientific procedure. To substitute an easy but imaginary problem for a difficult but real one, however, does not resemble true science so much as wishful thinking.

The experiment of suppressing value judgments, though a failure, does disclose something about human nature which refuses to remain concealed. Man is that creature who must have some criterion of the good. No man can wish to jump out of this situation without presupposing it; that is, without first judging that it would be "good" to do so. This means that the true realist is the man who acknowledges the distinction between good and evil and with it the category of sin.

CHAPTER III

HUMAN FREEDOM: TO THE GREEKS, FOOLISHNESS

Thou hast hid these things from the wise and prudent, and revealed them unto babes.

—Matthew 11:25

The impossibility of suppressing value judgments suggests that they are rooted in human nature, the reflection of some important constituent of it. They are in fact the expression of human freedom. Imagine that human freedom is a fiction, and value judgments automatically become meaningless. Conversely, try to deny the distinction between good and evil, and you are *ipso facto* in a world which knows no freedom. Therefore, if value judgments cannot consistently be denied, neither can the freedom upon which they depend. Consequently, the widespread deprecation of value judgments, described in the preceding chapter, entails an assault upon human freedom itself. The present chapter will show how the attack has often been spear-headed by the fields of science and philosophy.

This is all the more astonishing in view of the fact that science and philosophy represent supreme expressions of human freedom. The explanation, however, is fairly simple. It lies in one single assumption which these disciplines inherit from a common source: the assumption of ancient Greek scientists and philosophers that to every question "Why?" it must be possible to give an answer in *causal* terms. To the question, "Why did Socrates refuse to escape from prison?" this position is obliged to reply by resolving Socrates's actions into various causal factors. Human freedom is thereby ruled out in advance. By a subtle transition, as fateful in effect as it is harmless in appearance, the search for causes, in itself so constructive, has thus been converted into a dogma: the assumption that the specialized methods of science and philosophy, instead of being useful tools for the solution of certain kinds of problems, can actually solve them all. The man who subscribes to this article of faith is a determinist. With him the quest for knowledge, which ought properly to be a liberating enterprise, has become authoritarian. When he encounters questions that cannot be answered by the methods of logic or laboratory, he either dismisses them as meaningless or else subtly transposes them into other terms. But these are precisely the questions raised by the fact of freedom. If man really is free, then his behavior cannot be exhaustively explained in causal terms. The strong emphasis on human freedom, which is presupposed by almost everything the Bible says, is therefore, to adapt St. Paul's words, "foolishness to the Greeks." The following pages will illustrate how the determinist has historically engaged in a fairly constant attempt to deny human freedom. They will also show that he has done so, not so much from a completely disinterested regard for truth, as in the service of his dogma. His prior commitment to causal explanation restricts him to certain limited methods and therefore prescribes in advance the kind of answer he is permitted to discover.

THE DETERMINIST'S REPROACH AGAINST FREEDOM

The first embarrassing question which freedom poses to the open-minded intellectual is that of value judgments. If freedom is a fact, then one inevitably asks, "What is *worth* doing?" The quest for *the* good, as distinct from all merely apparent goods, becomes an urgent one. But this question is intractable to the methods of both scientist and philosopher. Their attempts to deal with it have consequently oscillated between the horns of a dilemma. On the one hand they have tried to establish some conception of the good on the basis of an irrefutable rational proof. On the other hand, discovering that all such proof can invariably be refuted by the same rational methods, they have tried the alternative of avoiding the question of values altogether. Experiments of this kind, however, as illustrated in the previous chapter, are foredoomed to futility. The question of values can neither be solved by intellectual means nor consistently suppressed. With a sound instinct intellectuals have realized that the root of their discomfiture is the fact of freedom. If they could only eliminate this troublesome reality, they would thereby abolish the possibility of value judgments as well. Hence the ambiguous status of freedom in some philosophic and scientific world views, and hence the direct attack upon it by many more.

The second reason why freedom is awkward to the intellectual is that it introduces an element of uncertainty and unpredictability into human action, an "x factor" which in principle could never yield to complete rational analysis. For knowledge, in the academic sense, is knowledge of causes, while freedom is irreducible to a completely determined sequence of cause and effect. It constitutes an unanalyz-able residue which will forever frustrate the aim of abstract knowl-edge. Hence the attempt of both scientist and philosopher to trans-pose questions about human behavior into questions answerable in terms of causes, whether "natural" or "logical."

The third embarrassment with which the fact of freedom confronts the ambitions of "pure reason" has plagued philosophers since the time of Socrates. If man really is free, then it follows that, although he may perceive the right, he may nevertheless will to do wrong. In that case the vaunted knowledge by which both scientist and phi-losopher hope to solve human problems would by itself be inadequate to the task. Assuming, for the sake of argument, that the true good could be rationally established, men would still be quite free to do the opposite. Philosopher and scientist would then be obliged to grant that their respective disciplines, though perhaps indispensable, were insufficient of themselves to solve life's most serious problems. Knowledge alone would provide no salvation.

Although in principle nothing prevents their recognizing that some problems are too big for syllogism or test tube, in practice it may become a matter of pride to deny it. The classic example is Socrates's dictum that "no man knowingly does evil." Although other philosophers, notably Aristotle, have seen that such a state-ment destroys human responsibility, they likewise have been too committed to "salvation by knowledge" to improve upon it. At this point the Bible agrees with ordinary common sense. The man who has to deal with the immediate, practical situations of everyday life knows intuitively that men frequently fail to act according to what they know to be right. In fact, nearly everybody knows this. Only to the determinist is it hidden.

In a significant magazine article several years ago a scientist re-corded his perplexity on pondering the discrepancy between his laboratory theories and his own behavior. He rightly concluded that if the theory of determinism were correct it should be applicable in practice. He therefore devised an experiment by which to test it.

On leaving his laboratory one evening he drove through the first red light he encountered. Stopped by the police, he patiently ex-plained that traffic fines were based upon the obsolete notion of human responsibility, whereas science had established that man's deeds are all causally determined. On being given an opportunity to repeat his plea to the judge he was asked,

"Are you then not responsible for what you do?"

"No."

"Very well," said the judge, "we are acquainted with cases of this sort. In fact, the state has provided an institution for people like yourself. Officer, take this man to the asylum." At this point the scientist decided that the theory of determinism had failed to pass the test.[1]

An equally revealing incident occurred at a recent discussion among members of a college faculty. A professor of psychology declared that the only hope for the solution of the world's problems was the extension of education and knowledge. Our trouble, he said, is that we still lack sufficient knowledge of how we ought to behave if we are to achieve our common goal. "But," demurred the professor of religion, "man is that creature who, even though he may know what he ought to do, can still do otherwise."

"Oh," retorted the psychologist, "original sin again."

"No," was the answer, "simply human freedom."

This exchange illustrates perfectly the gulf that separates biblical thinking from determinism. For the Bible, the mere *capacity* to know the right but do the wrong is no sin. Rather, it is the precondition of the greatest good. It places the highest premium on goodness done voluntarily, rather than by compulsion. From within the framework of the determinist's creed, however, this same freedom, the very image of God, is regarded as sin!

ATTEMPTS TO BANISH FREEDOM

In view of the several ways in which the fact of freedom constitutes an affront to the determinist's creed, it is no surprise to discover in the history of philosophy and science a persistent campaign against it. The attack is not always obvious. Philosophers like Spinoza or Hegel, for example, make considerable use of the word "freedom." A second look, however, reveals that they have redefined it beyond recognition. They both regard it as the mere "recognition of necessity." How far this is from the ordinary meaning of the word is evident from Spinoza's pronouncement that, if a stone hurtling through the air were endowed with consciousness, it would imagine that it was free.[2]

[1] See G. H. Estabrooks, "Tell it to the Traffic Cop," in *Harper's Magazine*, Vol. 157, November 1928, pp. 777–79. I owe this reference to Professor J. Howard Howson, of Vassar College.

[2] Benedict Spinoza, Epistle 62.

A philosopher like Henri Bergson, on the other hand, devotes much of his writing to refuting these deterministic theories and championing the cause of freedom. What emerges, however, is still not the faculty for responsible action, but only the spontaneous release of energy. In such a system animals turn out to be more free than man, since their energy can be released without the interference of rational considerations.

In the philosophy of existentialists like Martin Heidegger and Nicolas Berdyaev, both of whom make a great point of freedom, the definition flits from the Hegelian to the Bergsonian usage and back again, only rarely hovering for a moment at the common-sense meaning of the word.

As a possible exception to this philosophical tendency, the name of Immanuel Kant comes to mind. He was both a very great philosopher and also an ardent defender of freedom. There is certainly no doubt that he did believe in freedom as the capacity for responsible choice. But the question remains, is there any room for such freedom within the framework of a philosophical system so completely dedicated to the determinist's dogma as his? It obliges him to maintain that every event in the visible, material world happens according to a rigid necessity. Nothing could happen otherwise than it does. Such a world has no place for freedom, and he therefore quite consistently banishes it to the so-called "noumenal" realm, completely separated from the everyday world of space and time. A freedom that has no effect within this world remains, not just "noumenal," but merely *nominal*. It is quite true that Kant sometimes speaks as though freedom did have effect within the spatiotemporal world. When he does so, however, he sacrifices the consistency of his system. Instead of constituting an exception to the general philosophical tendency, his philosophy therefore only illustrates it more distinctly. He cannot provide for freedom without violating the determinist's creed.

Upon discovering the life-denying implications of these so-called "idealistic" philosophies, the modern humanist recoils. In search of an ally in his humanitarian concern he turns for help to science. He derives assurance from the fact that, while the philosopher's antagonism to all external relations drives him to negate the everyday world, the scientist acknowledges no other. His experimental method commits him irrevocably to experience. Bent on fathoming the secrets of the universe, the scientist has little patience with the other-worldly implications of a great deal of philosophy. He sees that their effect is sometimes to seduce men away from the real business of living and into a world of dreams.

The humanist who looks to science as his champion against the belittling of human concerns is doomed to disappointment. For science, though essentially not antihuman at all, can readily become so. This happens whenever the search for causes is subtly converted into the dogma that all occurrences, human behavior included, must be causally explainable. When this fateful transition is made, human freedom is precluded. And whoever is the enemy of freedom is ultimately the enemy of man. Spokesmen for science in the field of philosophy (that is, the empirical school) are indeed far more outspoken in their denial of freedom than the more traditional philosophers. Their rejection of it is unequivocal. Bertrand Russell, for example, while granting that the case is not susceptible of absolute proof, nevertheless holds that all human actions are predictable links in the series of cause and effect. Man, he says, like any other animal, is completely subject to the laws of nature. This thoroughgoing determinism, he grants, is the working assumption of the scientist.[3] C. D. Broad, another philosopher of science, concludes, in his incisive installation lecture at Cambridge, that freedom is a "delusive notion."[4]

Although neither of these two philosophers is a declared misanthrope (discounting the cynical tone of Russell's recent writings), it is only because neither has consistently adhered to the implications of his position. As often happens, the ultimate issue of a particular dogma is less apparent to those who hold it than to those who do not. In our day the warning has been sounded by artists and poets, like the one who wrote:

> Truth is a rope.
> It runs from the straining hands of man
> Up over a beam in the foundations of infinity,
> And binds its other end around his neck,
> Making of him as he stubbornly climbs from the earth
> His own inescapable hangman.[5]

[3]Bertrand Russell, op cit., pp. 125, 166, and 167.

[4]C. D. Broad, *Determinism, Indeterminism, and Voluntarism* (Cambridge, England: Cambridge University Press, 1934), p. 11.

[5]Quoted without reference by Max Otto, *Science and the Moral Life* (a Mentor Book published by the New American Library, 1949), p. 103.

Aldous Huxley's *Brave New World* is one of the best-known prophecies of what the scientific creed could do to man, while T. S. Eliot and W. H. Auden have put a similar warning into poetry.

A recent motion picture illustrated beautifully the steps by which a denial of human freedom leads inexorably to the degradation of man: *The Thing*, in which a military outpost near the North Pole is terrorized by a "thing" from outer space which lives on blood. An eight-foot, ambulatory vegetable in human form, and indifferent to bullets, it manages with diabolical cunning to corner the entire crew in what appears to be a certain deathtrap. The commander's desperate device for destroying the monster was nearly foiled at the last minute by the sudden intervention of the expedition's scientist. Drawing a gun on the rest of the company, he announces that, since the most important thing in the world is knowledge, it is their plain duty at all costs to communicate with the adversary and record whatever information it might impart. To this lofty end the sacrifice of their own lives might be regrettable but necessary. "Besides," he adds in perfect consistency, "it is a far superior creature to us. *It has no heart.*" Whether intentionally or not the film demonstrated how the man who makes knowledge an end in itself can forget that science was made for man and not *vice versa*. It added an ironic touch when, in his attempt to communicate with the heartless "thing," the most effective overture which the scientist could imagine was: "We're your friends."

In justifiable alarm at the inhuman implications of determinism, some scientists have hastened back to the laboratory in search of evidence for freedom. Significantly, however, they look for it not in man but in electrons. What they discover is consequently not freedom but merely the scientific version of the kind of "freedom" represented in philosophy by Bergson; that is, purposeless caprice. This is all that can be squeezed out of Heisenberg's famous principle of indeterminacy. Although this may be distinguishable from determinism, it is equally as remote from freedom. What the scientist is really looking for is self-determinism. He will never find it in electrons.[6]

Until recently the humanist trusted science to secure the pre-eminence of human concerns against the world-sick yearnings of so much philosophy. But today he is taking a long second look and does not

[6]An account of the indeterminacy which the scientist does discover in atomic physics is contained in Arthur H. Compton's *The Freedom of Man* (New Haven: Yale University Press, 1935).

like what he sees. He remembers that the inhuman atrocities of Communism are quite consistent with its boast of being the most scientific society in the world, the only one to rid itself completely of "bourgeois sentimentalism." The contemporary humanist is discovering in alarm that if Western scientists blench at such outrages it is often *in spite of* the inherent logic of their premises, rather than *because of* it. There is, for instance, nothing incompatible between concentration camps and the following statement by the renowned natural scientist, Sir Arthur Keith: "Nature keeps her human orchard healthy by pruning. War is her pruning hook."[7]

THEOLOGY'S COMPROMISE

Christian theology, which is in the strongest position to rebut the grim consequences of a consistent application of the "determinist's creed," has in fact frequently compromised with it. In his eagerness to make Christianity intellectually respectable, the theologian has attempted to reconcile Christianity with the monumental metaphysical systems which were part of the legacy of Greece to the medieval and modern world. His mistake lay, not in trying to make sense of Christianity, but in his uncritical assumption that the philosophy of Plato or of Aristotle comprises the last word in a rational account of man and his world. As a result, theology became wedded to a kind of thinking which denies many of biblical Christianity's truest insights, most of which are traceable to an unerring appreciation of human freedom. Although few if any theologians ever capitulated completely to this alien outlook, many did compromise with it. Consider, for example, the crucial question of whether men do evil voluntarily. The watershed which separates Greek from Hebraic thinking is summed up in the contrast between Socrates's claim that no man knowingly does evil and St. Paul's declaration that men "are without excuse, because, when they knew God, they glorified Him not as God, neither were they thankful" (Romans 1:20,21). The latter presupposes freedom, while the former precludes it. Yet a distinguished contemporary denies any substantial difference between these two outlooks and even brands as "cheap" any attempt to call attention to it.[8]

More often than not, Christian theology has been equivocal in its

[7]Quoted in the New York *Times*, January 8, 1955, p. 13.
[8]See Paul Tillich, *Systematic Theology*, Vol. I (University of Chicago Press, 1951), p. 95.

estimate of freedom. The classic example is the famous contention of St. Augustine that, while it is indeed a great freedom to be able to sin, it is a still greater freedom to be unable to sin (*non posse peccare*).[9] Precluding as it does the act of choice, such a "freedom" receives its name only by an abuse of words. When stripped of its misleading label, it turns out to be merely a disguised version of the determinist's ideal of complete predictability. Under the persistent influence of this unbiblical bias, Christian theology itself has sometimes regarded human freedom, not as the greatest gift of God, but as something to be overcome in the next world.[10]

If human freedom is not particularly desirable anyway, there is nothing objectionable about the famous theory of predestination. Four of the very greatest names in the history of Christian thought, Augustine, Thomas Aquinas, Luther, and Calvin, have all held this doctrine. Although they may differ somewhat in their formulation of it, they all maintain it in such a form as to preclude freedom. If it is objected that in other passages they assume freedom, this simply shows that they, no more than other thinkers, are able consistently to suppress the fact.

The argument most commonly urged in support of predestination is that, if man were free, this would detract from the majesty of God. Any defense of freedom automatically convicts itself of a presumptuous attempt to usurp divine prerogatives. But what if he willed to create individuals independent of himself and capable of responding freely to him? Within the terms of the argument under consideration, he would have to apply to the theologian for a permit. And his application would be rejected!

WISER THAN MEN

Under the influence of the "determinist's creed," men have tried to think and act as though there were no human freedom. No true fact, however, can be consistently denied, and this is what makes their failure so revealing. Whoever ignores or suppresses truth will be caught in an eventual self-contradiction. This is the last laugh which

[9]See, for example, St. Augustine, *The City of God*, Book XXII, Chapter 30.
[10]One of the shining exceptions is Sören Kierkegaard, who in some passages, at least, fully appreciates that the entire difference between biblical and other forms of thought hinges upon its affirmation of freedom. See, for example, Sören Kierkegaard, *Philosophical Fragments*, translated by David F. Swenson (Princeton University Press, 1946), pp. 61f.

truth enjoys at the expense of all misconceptions of it. Accordingly, whoever tries to exorcise freedom from one area of his thinking thus finds it grinning over his shoulder in another.

Obliged by these inconsistencies to acknowledge that freedom is no imaginary bogey, but still unwilling to come to terms with it, he yearns for a world which would correspond more closely to the "determinist's creed." In former times he sought it in a "higher" world of platonic ideas. Today he is more apt to seek it in a "brave, new world" under the dictatorship of science; that is, to take matters into his own hands and *make* the wayward creature, man, behave "rationally," which is to say, predictably.

In contrast with so many other theories, whether philosophical or scientific, the Bible consistently acknowledges human freedom. It is presupposed by all its key words, such as sin, repentance, forgiveness, love, and covenant. Consequently, though not intentionally philosophical, it contains by inference what is probably the most thorough understanding ever written of what it means to be a free agent. If, as the present book tries to show, the denial of freedom ultimately frustrates the intellectual pursuits in whose name it is denied, then, on purely rational grounds, the Bible must enjoy a distinct advantage over most other systems. This is one more variation on St. Paul's thesis that "the foolishness of God is wiser than men."

CHAPTER IV

HOMO RELIGIOSUS

> Choose ye this day whom ye will serve.
> —Joshua 24:15

The starting point for "biblical philosophy" is the recognition that judgments of good and evil are a constitutional necessity for every human being; that they are the inevitable concomitant of the exercise of free decision; and that the attempt either to avoid "value words" or to deny the fact of freedom must therefore ultimately be self-defeating. Though no affront to reason, this position does acknowledge the kind of question which, though unavoidable, might not be answerable either by the deductive method of philosophy or the inductive method of science. It has consequently given offense wherever men have pledged their total allegiance to either of these methods. Such a prior commitment obliges them to rule out in advance all questions which their respective methods are incapable of answering.

DEFINITION OF THE TERM "GOD"

The value judgments which free choice entails are "objective" in the sense that they refer to a standard of good and evil independent of oneself. They are distinguished from private inclinations and tastes by the fact that this external criterion can overrule personal preferences. If a man's value judgments are consequent upon the particular standard which he adopts, and if he cannot make a responsible decision without reference to it, the conclusion is that the very exercise of freedom necessarily involves the agent in a relation to something beyond himself. Every man alive, by virtue of his freedom, must have some such focal point to which he stands in acknowledged or unacknowledged relation. Even such a cynic as Adolf Hitler, who claimed to be a law unto himself, superior to external constraint, could not avoid appealing to the standard of "blood and soil." The conclusion reached in Chapter II, that "man is that creature who cannot avoid distinguishing good from evil," thus leads to the explanatory formula: The exercise of freedom always involves the agent in a relation to some criterion of value beyond himself.

The most important question that can be asked about a man
therefore is, "What is the external criterion upon which his judgments of good and evil depend?" The answer to this question will
shape all his decisions and thus the quality of his entire life. It would
therefore never occur to the biblical writers to record the biography
of a man (or a nation) apart from the point of reference toward
which his freedom is oriented, or—to use their technical term—his
"god." Taken by itself, this word carries as little specific meaning as
the word "good." Both are empty receptacles whose content varies
from man to man and from religion to religion. They are *functional*
words, the linguistic reflection of the fact that man is that creature
who, in the exercise of his freedom, necessarily appeals to some
criterion of good and evil. To ask *whether* a man believes in "God"
is consequently to misunderstand the issue. The proper question, as
the biblical writers never forget, is rather: What (or *who*) is his god?
As Martin Luther succinctly puts it, "Whatever, then, thy heart
clings to and relies upon, that is properly thy god."[1]

The issue can also be confused by the opposite misunderstanding:
the notion that, since every man has *a* god, all men therefore acknowledge the *same* god under different names. To use a favorite
metaphor of proponents of this view, everyone is climbing toward
the summit of the same spiritual mountain, and it is therefore foolish
to quarrel over whose route is the best. The most recent affirmation
of this position is made by Arnold Toynbee, who believes that the
four higher religions of today are "four variations on a single theme,
and that, if the four components of this heavenly music of the
spheres could be audible on earth simultaneously, and with equal
clarity, to one pair of human ears, the happy hearer would find himself listening, not to a discord, but to a harmony."[2]

The fallacy of this position consists in the assumption that, since
the rival deities all wear the same functional label ("god"), they are
at bottom identical. This is like saying that, because Henry VIII and
Louis XIV were both kings, they are fundamentally the same. Part
of the appeal of this position consists in the fact that it pretends to
a universal tolerance. In fact, however, it is really an adroit piece

[1] Martin Luther, "Larger Catechism," in *Luther's Primary Works* (London: Hodder & Stoughton, 1896), p. 34.
[2] Arnold J. Toynbee, *A Study of History* (Oxford University Press, 1954), Vol. 7,
p. 428. The most recent in a perennial flood of books on this subject is Frith Jof
Schuon's *Transcendent Unity of Religions*, trans. by Peter Townsend (New York:
Pantheon Books, 1953).

of propaganda on the part of one particular god: the undifferentiated unity of mysticism in which all contraries merge.[3] In spite of its manifest difficulties, this error, nurtured and cherished by idealistic philosophy, will always enjoy a wide popular appeal, since it offers the comforting assurance that life's most urgent question can be safely ignored: namely, "Which is the *true* God?"

To him who will not hear this question the Bible remains a closed book. It proceeds from the recognition that life is indeed a "battle of the gods" or, to put it more exactly, a battle between the true God and a host of pretenders. Hence the famous words of Elijah, "If Yahweh be God, then follow him; but if Baal, then follow him" (I Kings 18:21); or of the Book of Deuteronomy: "I call heaven and earth to witness against you this day, that I have set before thee life and death, the blessing and the curse; therefore choose life, that thou mayest live . . . to love the Lord thy God, to obey his voice, and to cleave unto him, for he is thy light, and the length of thy days" (Deuteronomy 30:19,20).

These passages express beautifully the biblical understanding that, simply by virtue of his native freedom, every human being is involved in a primordial commitment to one or another of these rival gods. It follows, moreover, that only one can be the *true* God. To suppose the contrary would be self-contradictory, since to the same question there cannot be two mutually exclusive answers. This means that the central problem of human life is precisely what the prophets said it was: the worship of false gods. The graven images against which the prophet inveighed are, from the twentieth-century perspective, absurd. It seldom occurs to modern men that idolatry is just as much alive today as it was twenty-five hundred years ago. If anything, it has become even more of a menace since it has learned to conceal itself. Unrecognized perils are always the most dangerous. The sophisticated "-isms" and "-ologies" in which modern man puts his trust simply function as graven images in modern dress.

By contrast to the favorite intellectual definition of man as *homo sapiens*, or rational animal, the prophets understand man as *homo religiosus*, religious animal. On this definition it is meaningless to distinguish between religious and nonreligious areas of life or between religious and irreligious men. He who rejects one religion (or god)

---

[3]This god has found a new and eloquent spokesman in W. T. Stace, whose *Time and Eternity* (Princeton University Press, 1952) is an excellent modern restatement of the attractive powers of this particular god.

can only do so in the name of another. Whereas to the Bible (and, in fact, to common sense generally) these are self-evident truths, the intellectual often has to rediscover them by hacking his way through a tangle of sophisticated error. He frequently never does win his way back to the point where biblical thinking begins.

If he does grant the foregoing reasoning, however, he may be due for a surprise. It entails a corollary which may be more than he bargained for: the biblical conception of sin! For sin is simply another word for allegiance to a false god. It is interchangeable with the word "idolatry." Hence, Christian theology often equates it with unbelief, not in the sense of "incredulity," but of trust in the wrong god.

The conception of sin as idolatry, though biblical in origin, is universal in application. As surely as he is free, every man will have a god. As surely as he has a god, he will have a conception of sin. He will be unable to deny any given version of it except in the name of another. He may disclaim the definition of sin as idolatry, but he can be overruled. Within the context of any given religious orientation, protests to the contrary notwithstanding, it can be shown that sin is really conceived in terms of defection to an alien "god," in the functional sense already indicated.

GENERAL AND SPECIFIC USAGES OF THE TERM "SIN"

The words "sin" and "idolatry" entail no definite content. Both are purely formal, words for which no man can avoid using some covert equivalent, but whose specific meanings will be as numerous as the rival gods. They only become specifically Christian with the biblical answer to the question, "Which is the *true* version of sin or idolatry?" And this, in turn, depends upon the prior question, "Which (or who) is the true God?"

A great deal of confusion has been caused by the failure to distinguish between the general and specific senses of "sin," "idolatry," and other words associated with Christianity. For example, it is often maintained that a piece of literature is informed by one of the "great Christian motifs" if it deals with the conception of sin (such as Robert Penn-Warren's *Brother to Dragons*), or salvation (such as Aldous Huxley's *Time Must Have a Stop*), or atonement (such as William Faulkner's *Requiem for a Nun*), or a savior (such as Faulkner's *A Fable*). Nothing could be further from the truth. There is nothing *specifically* Christian about any of these themes. Christianity merely understands, as many of its rivals do not, that they all stand for questions which arise the moment one acknowledges the fact of freedom. They are its corollaries. Even if the biblical answers were all wrong, if the biblical God were just another idol, these would still be demonstrably the right questions. Their hidden presence can be detected even in systems which deny them. Whether they can properly be called Christian will depend in each instance upon how they are *answered:* What is the specific conception of sin? Of what does salvation consist? Who accomplishes it, and how?

An example of the confusion which results from the failure to make this distinction is provided by even so acute a theologian as P. T. Forsyth, in his observations on Richard Wagner's opera, *Parsifal.* Because it does preach a doctrine of salvation from sin, and because it does have a savior, Forsyth supposes that it is to that extent a Christian drama.[4] Actually Wagner's avowed aim, expressly stated in many writings, was to replace Christianity by a substitute religion with himself as its prophet. He readily admitted that *Parsifal's* version of sin is the Hindu conception that human existence is itself a curse and that salvation consists in extinguishing all desires.[5] Nevertheless, when New York's Metropolitan Opera makes its annual gesture toward "religion" with a Good Friday performance of *Parsifal*, thousands of listeners continue to imagine that they are participating in a "great Christian experience." They thereby illustrate the contention of Denis deRougemont that Wagner's audiences have "a wonderful ability not to hear what is being sung."[6]

The word "sin," then, a purely formal word referring to the misorientation of human freedom, is no monopoly of Christianity. Every philosophy has its own conception of what man's external point of reference ought to be. Consequently, as the other side of the coin, it will also have its own conception of sin, though usually under a different name. The reason why it is mistakenly regarded as a "Christian motif" is simply that the Bible, adhering more rigorously

[4]See P. T. Forsyth, *Religion in Recent Art* (London: Hodder & Stoughton, 1905), the final two chapters, which deal with Wagner.

[5]See especially Wagner's two treatises, "Religion and the State" and "Religion and Art," in *Richard Wagner's Prose Works*, translated by W. A. Ellis (London: Kegan Paul, Trench, Trubner and Co., Ltd., 1897).

[6]Denis deRougemont, *Passion and Society* (London: Faber and Faber, Ltd., 1939), p. 231. The book is published in the United States under the title *Love in the Western World*.

than most other philosophies to the implications of human freedom, keeps the problem of sin in the foreground, instead of trying to circumvent it. Until one realizes that the issues with which it deals are *the* issues of human life, one will scarcely be interested in its specific answer to a question one has never faced. Conversely, when a man does awake to the fact that the discovery of the *true* God is a matter of life and death, he can hardly afford to ignore words like these:

For every one of the house of Israel, or of the stranger that sojourneth in Israel, which separateth himself from me, and setteth up his idols in his heart, and putteth the stumbling block of his iniquity before his face . . . I the Lord will . . . set my face against that man, and will make him a sign and a proverb, and I will cut him off from the midst of my people; and ye shall know that I am the Lord . . . That the house of Israel may go no more astray from me, neither be polluted any more with all their transgressions; but that they may be my people, and I may be their God, saith the Lord God (Ezekiel 14:7,8,11).

The distinctively biblical conception of sin thus depends upon the biblical conception of God and the effect which he exerts upon his worshipers. This will be examined in the following chapter.

CHAPTER V

THE HALLMARK OF IDOLATRY: A HARD HEART

> Where the Spirit of the Lord is, there is liberty.
> —2 Corinthians 3:17

Because man is free, he necessarily has as his "god" some criterion of decision independent of himself. This raises the problem of how to determine which of all the possible gods are only pretenders and which is the true One. The Bible applies a rigorous test. A false god can be detected by the fact that, having once become the repository of a man's allegiance, it straightway proceeds to destroy his freedom. Conversely, the true God preserves and enhances it.

THE PHILOSOPHER'S COMPLAINT AGAINST RELATEDNESS

Here again the Bible is at variance with the wisdom of the world. Most thinkers have contended that no god could pass this biblical test; that every "external reference" necessarily enslaves the individual; and that the only true freedom would consist in the absence of all relations to anything outside oneself. The burden of their argument is that a relation which fulfills freedom is a contradiction in terms. Is it not true, the philosopher asks, that one does feel every external relation as a limit, an actual or potential obstacle to one's will? Is not the only perfectly blessed state one of complete, unrelated self-sufficiency, void of any external relation whatever? Any point of reference external to oneself, he argues, automatically puts the self in subjection to an alien master. Any relationship in which one stands is, or may become, a ball and chain.

This refrain occurs again and again throughout the history of philosophy. Plato expresses it in these words: "The being who possesses good . . . has the most perfect sufficiency, and is never in need of anything else."[1] His follower Plotinus describes the mystical experience as one in which the soul leaves behind the chains which bind it to other things and attains to a state in which "she needs nothing more."[2] Aristotle concurs: "Happiness does not lack anything, but

[1] Plato, *Philebus*, paragraph 60.
[2] Plotinus, *Enneads*, VI, Chapter 9, paragraph 9.

is self-sufficient."[3] The same thought underlies the Stoic ideal of imperturbability, whose practical import is indicated by the famous words of Epictetus, "If you kiss your child or your wife, say to yourself that you are kissing a human being, for then if death strikes it, you will not be disturbed."[4] The Epicurean ideal of complete tranquillity is simply another version of the same thing, as Epicurus himself testifies: "Self-sufficiency is the greatest of all riches."[5]

So dear to the philosopher's heart is this ideal that he often appears to regard it as cheating to derive any bit of information, any aspect of his philosophical system, from a source outside himself. The following quotation from the philosopher Fichte illustrates the point beautifully:

The philosopher must deduce from his adopted principles all possible phenomena of experience . . . In the fulfillment of this purpose, he does not require the aid of experience; he proceeds *purely as a philosopher*, paying no respect whatever to experience; rather, he describes time as a whole in all its possible epochs, absolutely *a priori*.[6]

The inner logic of this drive to transcend all external relations is pressed to its relentless conclusion by the mystic. Since freedom necessarily relates a man to some criterion of judgment outside himself, the mystic concludes that the kind of freedom which men experience in everyday life is a counterfeit. It fools men into seeking their fulfillment outside themselves, whereas actually they are thereby taken prisoner.[7] True freedom must therefore be something quite different from the exercise of choice, decision, and purpose. It is, declares the mystic, simply a state of utter oneness. He will not even tolerate the question, "To what (or whom) shall I give my allegiance?" for any answer will involve the self in a hateful relation to the not-self. He attempts instead to transpose the question into the form, "How can I get rid of the tormenting freedom which binds me inexorably to some criterion outside myself, thereby permitting me only the mock liberty of choosing my own tyrant?" Though not widely known to an incredulous public, his answer has been ruthlessly consistent. He has

[3]Aristotle, *Nicomachean Ethics*, Book X, Chapter 6, paragraph 1176b, line 6.
[4]*The Manual of Epictetus*, aphorism 3.
[5]Epicurus, *Fragments*, aphorism 70.
[6]Quoted by F. M. Cornford, *The Unwritten Philosophy and Other Essays* (Cambridge University Press, 1950), p. 31. My italics.
[7]An eloquent statement of this position is contained in the article by Paul Tillich entitled "Two Types of Philosophy of Religion," *Union Theological Seminary Quarterly Review*, March 1946.

quite frankly admitted as his highest aspiration the annihilation of human freedom as we know it and consequently even of the human self. As the German mystic Tauler declares, "There remains to a man the fathomless annihilation of himself—of all aims, of all will, heart, purpose, or way."[8] The close kinship between contemporary existentialism and mystical philosophy is revealed by the famous comment of the existentialist Jean Paul Sartre, "Man is condemned to be free." The same sentiment is expressed more poetically by George Sand: "If I had found a man capable of dominating me, I should have been saved, for liberty is eating my life away and killing me. . . ."[9] The only difference between these two authors and a mystic like Plotinus is that they no longer believe in the possibility of the mystical ecstasy, in which one "ceases to be himself, he retains nothing of himself."[10]

This spite against one's own existence, so utterly contrary to the spirit of the Bible, has infiltrated Christian writings by way of the so-called Christian mystics. In the words of Meister Eckhart, "He alone hath true spiritual poverty [Eckhart's ideal] who wills nothing, knows nothing, desires nothing."[11] Biblical Christianity at least has within itself a solid point of leverage from which to attack such doctrines. The rest of the world, without defense against their sophisticated infection, has to an alarming degree succumbed. If the humanist finds Christianity antihuman, it is largely because it has uncritically absorbed an alien world view.

Although this philosophy splits into a thousand inconsistencies under close logical scrutiny, it nevertheless exerts a powerful emotional appeal. The sincere layman all too readily takes at face value the mystic's claim to have plumbed the depths of man's inner experience. In actual fact, however, instead of really *discovering* such sentiments in the human heart, he is far more apt to have planted them there himself. The mystic is a past master at sowing seeds of discontent with the everyday world where none existed before. His entire case is not really based upon an accurate description of human

[8]Mary F. Robinson, *The End of the Middle Ages* (London: P. Fisher Unwin, n.d.), p. 83.

[9]André Maurois, *Lélia, The Life of George Sand,* translated by Gerard M. Hopkins (New York: Harper & Brothers, 1953), p. 156.

[10]*The Philosophy of Plotinus,* edited by Joseph Katz (New York: Appleton-Crofts, Inc., 1950), p. 156.

[11]Cited by D. T. Suzuki, *Essays in Zen Buddhism,* first series (London: Luzac and Company, 1927), p. 364.

consciousness but upon the entirely preconceived notion that any relation beyond oneself must necessarily be felt as intolerable. The minds of those who are under his spell are closed in advance to the possibility that one very special kind of relation, instead of inhibiting or oppressing freedom, might actually fulfill it.

THE ONE RELATION WHICH LIBERATES

The actuality of such a unique relation is precisely what the Bible proclaimed. In view of the almost unanimous judgment of the Gentile world that such a relation is impossible, its claim was bound to sound like "foolishness to the Greeks." A measure of the extent to which our own generation is far more Greek than Christian is the fact that the biblical word for this unique relation is certain to be misunderstood. The Greek word which the New Testament uses, *agape*, has become impossible to translate into English. If rendered as "charity," it suggests almsgiving or the community chest; if as "love," one thinks of Hollywood or true-story magazines. In order to prevent such misunderstanding, the Greek word will be frequently used in the following pages.

The way in which *agape* actually does liberate the free agent instead of cramping his style can be illustrated by an experience common to most people. In any stimulating conversation, especially spirited dialogue between persons in love, each suddenly finds himself exercising unsuspected gifts of wit and insight which neither could generate by himself. The stimulus of creative interchange evokes resources which would otherwise have remained dormant. Although a remark by one party does indeed "condition" the other's reply, the effect of this "conditioning" is not negative but positive. Instead of circumscribing one's freedom, it provides the occasion for his own creative response. Instead of tyrannizing, it liberates.

This fact of experience confounds the preconceived notion that only in splendid isolation is one truly free. Such a "freedom," definable only in terms of what it is free *from*, obliterates the very structure of real freedom. The biblical alternative, on the contrary, preserves and accentuates it. One cannot talk meaningfully about the fulfillment of human freedom without preserving its relational character. While so many philosophies have therefore not talked about it meaningfully at all, the Bible proclaims that to live truly is to live in a relation of *agape* with one's fellows.

Against this the world brings three important objections. First, protests the realist, one must grant in all honesty that not a soul alive really does love his neighbor as himself. If taken seriously, this Christian precept is therefore irrelevant. At best it can be retained only as a frankly unattainable ideal which might serve nevertheless to moderate the ingrained selfishness of men.

Secondly, cries the voice of experience, if Christianity insists that human freedom can be fulfilled only in a particular kind of relation, why does it have to choose the one which has historically been the most disastrous of all, the relation of man to man? The testimony of the ages is one long chronicle of conflict and violence. It is matched at the personal level by the psychoanalyst's discovery that declarations of love may camouflage emotions of hostility which the individual has successfully hidden from himself. Beneath the surface even the most ostensibly affectionate family may conceal a state of undeclared warfare between its members. To go about practicing Christian love in such a world is therefore simply to invite people to take advantage of one. He who loves is vulnerable, whereas the secret of living is to become invulnerable. As for the claim that spirited conversation is an illustration of love, what more eloquent rebuttal than the recent satires of Stephen Potter? With an effect as devastating as it is humorous, his *Gamesmanship* and *Lifemanship* reveal that the art of conversation is in reality nothing but the technique for subtly squelching one's fellows. The only practical course is not to offer one's neighbor a target. Hence the advice of so many of the world's philosophies and religions is to fly from the persecution and contamination of society to the solitary life of the hermit.[12] Even many of history's most gregarious figures, like Byron or Casanova, have privately admitted a contempt for the men (and women) whose company they cultivated. They agreed with the recluse that the last place to look for personal fulfillment is the society of one's fellow man. In the words of Sartre's epigram, "Hell is other people."

Finally, according to the wisdom of the world, since love is a matter of the emotions, it is not subject to control by the exercise of will power. You cannot like somebody simply by concentrating on it. What could be more quixotic, therefore, than to lay down as a uni-

[12]So-called Christian mystics have often repeated this wholly unbiblical advice. The classic example is the contention of St. John of the Cross that love toward the neighbor impedes one's love for God. See E. Allison Peers, *The Complete Works of St. John of the Cross*, edited by P. Silverio De SantaTeresa (Westminster, Maryland: The Newman Press, 1953), Vol. 1, pp. 24, 43.

versal goal something that men could not achieve by their own efforts?[13]

THE DEARTH OF LOVE

To these objections the "biblical philosopher" makes the following reply. To the first, the complaint that men do not in fact love their neighbor as themselves, he reacts with a mixture of surprise and satisfaction. Surprise, because he is accustomed to the opposite charge: namely, that Christianity takes too dim a view of human nature to appreciate the extent of actual good will in the world. Satisfaction, because here at least is a point on which both he and his disputant can agree: the woeful absence of love from a world bent upon self-destruction. A nice symbol of this is the fact that *agape*, one of the most frequent words in the New Testament, occurs only about half a dozen times outside the Bible. Its sudden emergence in the gospels and epistles symbolizes the new reality which they proclaim, in contrast to the loveless "normalcy" to which the world has learned to accommodate itself.

This is precisely the situation which leads the psalmist to exclaim, "There is none that doeth good, no, not one" (Psalm 14:3). It has also prompted Christian theologians to coin the phrase at which his antagonist probably takes offense: "original sin." Even if this is not an entirely happy expression, on its best interpretation it simply stands for the very situation to which the critic himself has called attention.

The Christian, in short, is the last person who needs to be reminded, whether by psychiatrist or cynic, of man's inhumanity to man. On the contrary, he is in a position to chide the wisdom of the world with not going far enough. The fate which the world metes out to perfect *agape* could hardly be more poignantly symbolized than by a religion whose emblem is the cross. The self-styled realist has no stomach for so thoroughgoing a realism. As he silently takes his leave, the Christian is at least justified in one parting request:

[13]In an abortive attempt to answer this complaint some Christians are currently saying that, while one cannot *like* everybody, one can *love* everybody, because Christian love does not concern the emotions. In addition to being unbiblical, this position succeeds only in making the kingdom of heaven a rather grim and unattractive place. Although this misunderstanding is fairly common, its most powerful impetus has come from the celebrated book by Anders Nygren, *Agape and Eros*, translated by Philip F. Watson (London: S.P.C.K., 1953).

that he never again be accused of wishful thinking or sentimental illusions.

THE VULNERABILITY OF LOVE

The second objection was that, of all conceivable relations, none can become more intolerable than that between man and man, and that anyone naïve enough to put love into practice would simply invite the world to abuse him. The counsel of prudence is therefore to withdraw from society into the perfect invulnerability of solitude. The Christian replies that, although there is indeed nothing more crippling and destructive than negative human relations, this in itself suggests that they possess a unique potency. It is a matter of common experience that the things which can do the most harm, whether knowledge, or money, or atomic energy, can also exert the highest potency for good. It is therefore not unreasonable to expect that, like the energy of the atom, human relations too, under the right conditions, might be the greatest constructive force there is. This expectation is emphatically corroborated by the results of contemporary psychotherapy, which finds, on the one hand, that a hostile human environment is the principal cause of neurosis and, on the other hand, that being treated with respect and dignity is indispensable to the patient's cure.

Psychotherapy also corroborates with clinical evidence the contention that human speech can do every bit as much damage to personality as physical torture. It can be subtly used to annihilate a person without actually breaking the rules of decorum. Who has not heard the word "darling" used as a poisoned dart? From the analyst's couch come endless variations on this theme. Small wonder that men fly from human company and seek refuge in the wilderness, for nature cannot talk back. Nevertheless, the same psychiatrists also make human speech the very cornerstone of the therapeutic process. It is precisely through a positive "conversational relation" with the analyst that the patient is progressively healed. According to a recent book on the subject, nothing is more important for maintaining or regaining mental health than being able to converse freely with someone who can be trusted not to take advantage of one's vulnerability. It is not just a useful doctor's device but a prerequisite of continuing sanity.[14]

[14]Harry and Bonaro Overstreet, *The Mind Alive* (New York: W. W. Norton & Co., Inc., 1954), Chapter 2.

Thus human intercourse generally, and speech specifically, can be used with deadly effect but can also become the most potent force for good. Although one can appreciate the hermit's conclusion that to save himself he must abandon society and live a life of silence, his logic is fallacious.[15] What is most disastrous when wrongly used, like a knife in the hand of an assassin, might still be the only thing that would save a man—in the hand of a surgeon. The fateful power of words, as the primary medium of human relationships, has not been more decisively stated than this:

Out of the abundance of the heart the mouth speaketh. The good man out of his good treasure bringeth forth good things, and the evil man out of his evil treasure bringeth forth evil things . . . For by thy words shalt thou be justified, and by thy words shalt thou be condemned. (Matthew 12:34-37.)

The objection also contains another misunderstanding, the notion that each man is an isolated unit whose salvation would have to be entirely independent of his fellows and what they might do. Such a conception is incompatible with *agape*. It is not a unilateral relation but a reciprocal one; not something which I radiate in sublime independence of my neighbor but rather a relation of a certain quality between myself and him. Where there is only one person there can be no *agape*.

It may be objected that the love of God himself is completely unilateral, remaining the same regardless of whether or not it is returned. This is to forget that the Old Testament is the history of God's unrequited and therefore disappointed faithfulness to an idolatrous people. "All the day long have I stretched out my hand unto a rebellious people . . . a people that provoketh me to anger continually to my face" (Isaiah 65:2,3). Exactly the same point is made by the New Testament parables of the one lost sheep and of the lost coin, whose owner is grieved until he recovers them. The Bible is quite clear from beginning to end that its God is one whose love does not reach fulfillment until it is reciprocated.

Since love is a multilateral relation, the Bible's primary concern is not with the individual in isolated meditation, nor even with the sacrifice of oneself to the human beast of prey, but with men in community and the mutual relations between them. *Two* or *three* must be gathered before the Lord is present in their midst. This is reflected

[15]It is difficult to see how the vow of silence taken by certain Christian monks can be reconciled with the biblical outlook.

in the practice of churches like the Protestant Episcopal, Eastern Orthodox, and Roman Catholic, in which the priest may not say a mass if no one else is present. For the sake of emphasis, one might make the risky generalization that it is impossible to be either a Christian or a Jew by oneself. Even without the necessary qualifications this statement is still more true than its opposite. It confutes the definition of religion formulated by A. N. Whitehead and others that "Religion is what the individual does with his own solitariness." The trouble with this definition is that it does not include *biblical* religion. The pity is that so many Christians have been persuaded that it does.

The key to the reply to the objection under consideration is the Church. With the possible exception of "love," no word has undergone a greater change in meaning, or been subject to more misunderstanding, than this. Originally it referred to those between whom the relation of *agape* had been created. The New Testament word for it, *ecclesia*, derives from the verb "to call out" and means "the community of those who have been called out"—that is, called out of a loveless world into a re-created, redemptive company whose members are united by the bond of *agape*. A partial answer to the complaint that to practice love in a hostile world is suicidal is therefore this: The Christian is not called in the first instance to walk the plank for the amusement of a sadistic world but to enter a new kind of community, one which man cannot create by himself alone. St. Paul describes it in words borrowed from the Old Testament: "Come ye out from among them, and be ye separate . . . and I will receive you and be to you a Father, and ye shall be to me as sons and daughters, said the Lord Almighty" (2 Corinthians 6:17,18). Lest this separateness be misinterpreted as a parochial exclusiveness (as it has been construed by some sectarian groups), it should be added, first, that it is simply a description of experienced fact—the fact which caused the word *agape* to be retrieved from the bone yard and placed at the heart of the New Testament; and, second, that this same "datum" of experience is offered as a free gift to all who will accept it. The Church is in fact bound to impart it as widely as possible. Granted that it has often done so clumsily or not at all, nevertheless it is the world which rejects the Church more often than vice versa.

But the rest of the answer to this objection grants its grain of truth. In a sense the Christian will suffer at the hands of a non-Christian world. Rather than offering escape from the world, however, his religion impels him into it. Precisely because he knows the redemptive power of *agape*, he is all the more sensitive to its absence. Because his God is one who takes the world's tragedies upon himself, he too can enjoy no complacent luxuriating in salvation as long as the sins of men (pre-eminently his own) continue to write the history of the human race in blood. In contrast to the Stoic ideal of detached imperturbability, he does not seek immunity to the heartbreaks of the world. Rather, he is empowered to bear it by One stronger than he who has already triumphed over it. The fruit of this victory is a present reality in the redemptive community, the assurance of ultimate triumph beyond the ruin of any personal disaster. Martyrdom, though not often spectacular, and never cultivated for its own sake, is therefore not simply a phenomenon of the early Church, but something for which the Christian is ready at any time. If it comes, he is able by the grace of God to meet it without regret but rather in accordance with the apostolic injunction: "Inasmuch as ye are partakers of Christ's suffering, *rejoice*" (1 Peter 4:13), an exhortation which is indeed "foolishness" apart from the words of Christ, "In the world ye shall have tribulation: but be of good cheer; I have overcome the world" (John 16:33). This is the basis of the apostle's exalted assurance:

Who shall separate us from the *agape* of Christ? Shall tribulation, or distress, or persecution, or famine, or nakedness, or peril, or sword? Nay, in all these things we are more than conquerors through him who loved us. For I am persuaded that neither death, nor life, nor angels, nor principalities, nor powers, nor things present, nor things to come, nor height, nor depth, nor any other creature, shall be able to separate us from the *agape* of God, which is in Christ Jesus, our Lord (Romans 8:35–39).

THE IMPROBABILITY OF LOVE

The realist's third objection, that love is not something which can be engendered simply by the exertion of will power, can be answered in a single word: "Amen!" If human fulfillment were simply a matter of practicing a prescribed set of regulations, there would be no problem. Anyone, if he sets his mind to it, can fulfill the requirements of a legalistic code of conduct. As St. Paul says, in effect: Judged by the righteousness which is in the law, I was found blameless (see Philippians 3:6). To perform acts of benevolence from the right *motive*, however, is quite another thing. A plausible external facsimile of *agape* might be motivated instead by prudence, prestige, or self-righteousness. Although the power of self-control can accomplish great things, it frequently cannot govern motives. In short, the human situation has got too badly out of hand to be overcome by tugging at one's bootstraps. As Christ might well have said, "Which of you by taking thought can love his neighbor as himself?"

If any proof of God is to be found in the Bible it is the one implied by this question. He would be God indeed who could do the one thing man most desperately needs but cannot accomplish by himself. He can transform hardened hearts by evoking in them the power to love. On learning that the God of the Bible is willing to be accepted or rejected by this test, the skeptic blinks incredulously. And well he might, for he knows only too well that the ways of the world are not the ways of love. Both his amazement and his unbelief are precisely what one would expect, as St. Paul understood when he cited the Old Testament prophecy: "Behold, ye despisers, and wonder, and perish. For I work a work in your days, a work which ye shall in no wise believe, even though a man declare it unto you" (Acts 13:41). The mighty work of God which Paul declares to the skeptic is simply this: "The love of God is shed abroad in our hearts by the Holy Spirit which is given unto us" (Romans 5:5).

In the world at large, the wellsprings of *agape* are so nearly dry that its flickering appearance is continually at the mercy of the forces of fear and hostility in everyone. At a particular point in time, however, this situation was overcome by the agency of God himself. Although the *fact* that he has done this is one of the greatest mysteries, the way in which he does it is quite understandable. In ordinary human experience one loves as a result of having first *been* loved. The followers of Jesus were transformed into the Church because precisely this had happened to them. Once men had been loved unconditionally from beyond themselves, the vicious circle of hardheartedness was broken. To enter into this new and unique kind of community was to experience the liberating power of *agape* among its members.

Christianity stakes its claim, not upon the moral perfection of its members, but upon a concrete, down-to-earth datum. Its God is neither a vague abstraction nor a sublime ideal, but rather is known concretely as he who transforms hard hearts into a community of redemption. What was impossible for man by himself becomes a given fact by virtue of the prior love of God for all who will respond to it. Hence the declaration of St. John: "Herein is love, not that we loved God, but that he first loved us. We love, because he first loved us" (1 John 4:10,19).

The proof of Christianity is thus not to be captured in flights of speculative theory but is rooted in stubborn fact—the kind of fact which no amount of wishful thinking can either conjure up or exorcise, namely, the quality of man's relation with his neighbor. If it is governed by devotion to the impersonal ideal of "service" or "doing good," it is still a far cry from *agape*. And if it is informed by suspicion, envy, exploitation, resentment, vindictiveness, or emulation, this can indeed be camouflaged, not only from oneself, but from the neighbor. But, however effective the disguise, it cannot alter the reality. On the psychiatrist's couch the truth will out—often with greater violence than in the days when men regularly confessed their sins to God. Though one may not be proud of these emotions, they are nevertheless concrete, intractable data. The attempt to banish them by an act of will only drives them further underground, where they continue to operate silently toward one's own undoing. The psychiatrist finds daily corroboration of this. As one has recently written, "Many people, of course, for reasons of expediency, fear, or conscience, manage to hold a reciprocal rage in check—and to pay for the effort later in the coin of headache, and fatigue. . . ."[16]

These stubborn facts drive the hermit to seek salvation through the severance of all personal ties, to insure against hostile emotions by cultivating a state of neutrality. For that very reason they likewise provide the raw material for Christianity's strongest proof. Whereas with man it is impossible to convert neutral and negative emotions into the concrete fact of *agape*, with God all things, even this most improbable miracle, are possible. If a man should encounter someone who could actually do this, who could transform a hardened heart, he would know that he was dealing with the Almighty God. Hence the constant biblical emphasis on the radical difference between "before" and "after," a difference so great that Saul, no longer able to regard himself as wholly the same person, changed his name to Paul. The Bible's meaning is terribly literal when it speaks of it as the difference between death and life. How correct it is can be substantiated by the following thumbnail proof.

[16]H. and B. Overstreet, op. cit., p. 248.

If man is a free agent, then to annihilate his freedom, as the mystic would do, is obviously death to the individual. Likewise, if his freedom always puts him in relation to a criterion beyond himself, which in turn puts his freedom in bondage, the result is the gradual extinction of the self. Hence to worship a false god is literally a living death. And conversely, if there is any true life at all, it could only consist in a relation to Someone who, however unexpectedly, fulfills a man's freedom instead of destroying it. These are the considerations, indeed the facts, from which is derived the formula: either suicide or God.

How utterly antithetical this biblical answer is to most philosophical and religious speculation is beautifully illustrated by the following quotation, which expresses the ultimate issue of mysticism:

Do not get yourselves entangled with any object, but stand above, pass on, and be free. . . . Do not be deceived by others . . . if you encounter any obstacles, lay them low right away. If you encounter the Buddha, slay him; if you encounter the Patriarch, slay him; . . . slay them all without hesitation: for this is the only way to deliverance.[17]

The contrast with the following biblical proclamation speaks for itself: "We know that we have been brought from *death* unto *life* because we *love* the brethren." (1 John 3:14. My italics.)

The Christian doctrine of sin can therefore be given a precise formulation in terms of its opposite. When man's freedom is oriented toward the true God, he no longer seeks fulfillment by taking advantage of his neighbor, nor by fleeing from him, nor by becoming impervious to him, nor by becoming his psychological slave. The true God is he whose power to evoke *agape* binds men together in a redemptive community. Conversely, pseudo gods, instead of fulfilling man's freedom, actually put him in bondage. The unmistakable mark with which they brand their victims is hardness of heart.

NOTE

The distinction made in this and the following chapters between motive and act could be misleading if it suggested that the two were completely separable. According to the Christian understanding of the unity of the personality, the motive always colors the act, how-

[17]These quotations from the famous Buddhist teacher Rinzai are quoted by D. T. Suzuki, *Essays in Zen Buddhism*, First Series (London: Luzac and Company, 1927), p. 332.

ever imperceptibly. Although an act of *agape* could be copied, it could never be exactly duplicated. The eye of the camera might fail to detect the imitation, but subtle differences in tone of voice, quality of gesture, and facial expression would give it away. This view is borne out both by psychiatric data and by everyday experience.

Part II
Partial Eclipse of the
Biblical Understanding of Sin

in which it is shown how the specifically biblical conception of sin has often been partly obscured by the intrusion into Christian thinking of the two pagan versions.

CHAPTER VI

SIN MISCONCEIVED AS BREAKING RULES

> By the works of the law shall no flesh be accounted righteous.
> —Galatians 2:16

The principal alternatives to the Christian conception of sin fall under two headings, to be discussed in this and the succeeding chapter. The first defines sin primarily as the breaking of rules, while the second regards it as due to some constituent element of human existence as such. Though each can be so stated as to express a fraction of the biblical view, they both do it more violence than justice. The unfinished task of Christian theology is to disentangle itself from these two alien versions of sin and to challenge them with the distinctive biblical one.

Two decisive turning points in the history of Christian thought were brought to a head over the question of whether or not sin could be exhaustively defined as the breaking of rules. These were the Protestant Reformation, in the sixteenth century, and the historic controversy between St. Augustine and the British monk Pelagius at the turn of the fourth century. The latter contended that sin was the failure to live up to moral laws. God had made perfectly clear through the Ten Commandments and the Sermon on the Mount what was required of man and how he ought to use his freedom. If he would, man could discipline himself to obey these rules and thereby earn God's favor and assistance in the perfection of his moral nature. It is at once evident that Pelagius's doctrines are still very much alive today. The man in the street, whether nominally a Christian or not, is apt to regard Christianity as essentially a kind of moralism. The difference between Christians and non-Christians appears to him to depend simply on whether one thinks that on the whole this system of "do's" and "don't's" benefits society or, with Dr. Kinsey, that its restrictions are irrelevant and harmful in the twentieth century.

The fundamental issue between biblical Christianity and any sort of moralism concerns the nature of God and consequently of the true fulfillment of human freedom. The real issue can only be joined when the implicit "theologies" underlying the respective conceptions of sin are brought into the open. The moralist's god is either a mythological lawgiver or an equally mythical "rational principle" projected onto the heavens and requiring human conformity. The biblical God, on the other hand, is Some*one*—a mighty personality before whose judgment the powerful tremble and whose love far transcends the quibbling calculation of *quid pro quo*. The favor of such a God is not for sale. If done from the wrong motive, no amount of good works can appease his wrath or purchase his love. He is dissatisfied with all such works until they are motivated by *agape*. His love embraces the total person and not just his deeds.

If this is the kind of God with whom man must reckon, then to define sin as the failure to perform certain good works is to mistake the symptom for its underlying cause. Sin is rather any orientation of the heart which destroys *agape*, and "bad works" simply its visible manifestation. To denounce them is no remedy at all. It only obscures, and may even aggravate, the real problem. If, however, these undesirable symptoms could be forgiven, the individual might experience a reorientation of the heart which alone could transform them.

But this is a very big "if," and it was too much for Pelagius. It meant that the individual did not have it in his power to save himself by his own effort alone. For love is a bilateral relation. One can neither establish *agape* nor achieve forgiveness by a unilateral act of will. This is the point at which the moralist will always balk. One may readily acknowledge that he is at least partly motivated by a genuinely Christian concern. He fears lest the denial of the efficacy of individual effort undercut two of the foundation stones of Christianity: its heightened sense of personal responsibility and its powerful moral incentive. Without these the common man is at the mercy (as he is today) of the sophisticated pagan philosophies of doubt, drift, and defeat.

THE HARDHEARTEDNESS OF MORALISM

Nevertheless, moralism of whatever sort, no matter how elevated, exerts a deadly effect upon the human spirit. It not only falls dismally short of the biblical understanding of righteousness, but actively inhibits and destroys *agape*, and does so precisely at the point which Pelagius considered the great asset of his position. The very ethical incentive for which he fought can actually become the most effective hardener of hearts. By ensnaring the individual in a morbid preoccupation with his own moral balance sheet, the very pursuit of goodness betrays him into a relentless scrupulosity. He becomes a veritable miser of the spirit, rendered more incapable of love with each halfpenny virtue that is jealously added to his hoard. Instead of regarding his neighbor with love, he too often sees every man as a potential competitor for righteousness toward whom he must at all costs establish himself as "holier than thou."

Competition for virtue, even more than competition for money, dries up the springs of sympathy and compassion. The lovelessness of the moralist has become proverbial in much of the world's great literature. In Victor Hugo's *Les Misérables*, Javert's passion for legal justice drives him to the lifelong persecution of one whose nobility of character stands in ironic contrast to his technical guilt before the law. Samuel Butler's *The Way of All Flesh* contains a vivid description of how emotional *rigor mortis* settles down upon a marriage governed by the letter of the law:

. . . after they had been married some twenty years Christina had somewhat fallen from her original perfection in money matters. She had got gradually in arrears during many successive quarters, till she had contracted a sort of domestic national debt, amounting to between seven and eight pounds. Theobald at length felt that a remonstrance had become imperative, and took advantage of his silver wedding day to inform Christina that her indebtedness was cancelled, and at the same time to beg that she would endeavor henceforth to equalize her expenditures and her income. She burst into tears of love and gratitude and assured him that he was the best and most generous of men, and never during the remainder of her married life was she a single shilling behind-hand.[1]

The story acquires a touch of pathos from the fact that both parties imagined that this blighted relationship was love. It also illustrates how the legalist's crusade for absolute justice turns out to be a campaign for psychological dominion over his neighbor. Whoever can be persuaded to take him seriously is automatically pitted against insuperable odds—for who has any right against the flaming sword of justice?

Nathaniel Hawthorne's *The Scarlet Letter* exposes the way in which the mask of virtue can provide the perfect disguise for unlovely motives. It discloses the secret gratification with which the Puritan denounces immorality and the vindictiveness with which he demands the miscreant's hide. Modern psychiatry reinforces biblical insights when it discovers the reason why the moralist takes such

[1]Samuel Butler, *The Way of All Flesh* (New York: Literary Classics Book Club, n.d.), p. 70.

pleasure in pointing the guilty finger. The intensity of his gratification reflects either the measure of his own inner hostility or the strength of his secret desire for the forbidden fruit which he condemns, while his show of outrage serves to hide this embarrassing fact from both himself and the world.

The Bible illustrates the cruelty of legalism through the medium of dramatic narrative, such as the account of the woman taken in adultery (John 8:1–11). Since the law required that she be stoned, her accusers sought to put Jesus in the position of either defying the law or acquiescing in her execution. But they reckoned without his observation, "He that looketh upon a woman to lust after her hath already committed adultery" (Matthew 5:28), and were consequently confounded by the quiet reply, "He that is without sin among you, let him cast the first stone." As they departed in silence, their own vindictiveness is contrasted with the attitude of Christ:

Woman, where are they? Doth no man condemn thee? And she said, No man, Lord. And Jesus said, Neither do I condemn thee. Go thy way, and from henceforth sin no more.

Jesus emphatically does not condone adultery or in any way minimize the significance of specific, concrete breaches of conduct. "Go and sin no more." But these acts are set in a context in which, upon a change of heart by the individual (repentance), the last word need not be retribution, but redemption. In his own words, "God sent not his Son into the world to condemn the world; but that the world through him might be saved." (John 3:17.)

THE HYPOCRISY OF MORALISM

This episode illustrates how moralism leads not only to hardheartedness but also to hypocrisy. Good works divorced from the motives behind them can become a highly perfected instrument for blinding oneself and deceiving others. A psychiatrist pricks up his ears on learning that his patient showers the members of his family with presents. It need not necessarily be so, but this may represent an attempt to compensate by external means for what money can never restore: broken and resentful emotional relations. In the same way any good work *may* be done from an ulterior motive. A financier's contribution to charity may be made simply for the sake of reputation; a diplomat's banquet may be intended to appease or ingratiate; a parent's self-denial may be exploited to induce in the child a hopeless sense of infinite indebtedness. These abuses are encouraged wherever good works are made into an end in themselves. The motives behind them being thereby exempt from criticism, they can operate without detection. As a contemporary writer puts it, "The cry of unselfishness often comes from those who, under the pretense of active philanthropy, are busily engaged in the violent, aggressive, dominating assertion of self, who, while they profess and perhaps believe that they are giving their lives to the service of others, are really using others in great part for their own glory."[2] The most eloquent exposé of the moralist, however, is again to be found in the Bible:

Woe unto you, scribes and Pharisees, hypocrites! For ye make clean the outside of the cup and of the platter, but within they are full of extortion and excess. Thou blind Pharisee, cleanse first that which is within the cup and platter, that the outside of them may be clean also. Woe unto you, scribes and Pharisees, hypocrites! For ye are like unto whited sepulchres, which indeed appear beautiful outwardly, but are within full of dead men's bones, and of all uncleanliness. Even so ye also outwardly appear righteous unto men, but within ye are full of hypocrisy and iniquity. (Matthew 23:25–28.)

The reason why Jesus sought the company of harlots, winebibbers, and sinners was not that he approved their ways. But, since they were not desperate to prove their own virtue, they still retained the two qualities without which no one can hear him. They could be honest with themselves, and they still had a heart.

THE TYRANNY OF MORALISM

The superiority of the biblical view of sin to the moralistic can be established on purely philosophical grounds. The main line of the argument is laid down by St. Paul in his Epistle to the Galatians. These recent Christian converts had already begun to lapse back into a religion of legal observances, in the vain attempts to subject *agape* to calculated control by individual effort. More concerned to expunge this error than to qualify each remark against misconstruction by future theologians, St. Paul shows how the moralist is really in contradiction with himself. Although his concern is to emphasize and preserve human freedom, his method of doing so has the opposite effect. When the "good life" is conceived as rigid obedience to an external law, the individual's freedom is forfeited. Such a life is

[2]Gamaliel Bradford, *Saints and Sinners* (Boston: Houghton Mifflin & Co., 1932), p. 118.

analogous to elections under a totalitarian regime, in which everybody may cast a ballot but is subject to penalty for not voting the official line. As long as liberty is merely the freedom to knuckle under to an external authority, then rebellion will always appear the greater freedom.[3]

Hence St. Paul is at pains to distinguish Christianity from any "law of commandment contained in ordinances" (Ephesians 2:15). "By the works of the law shall no flesh be accounted righteous" (Galatians 2:16), not simply because the law does not happen to be sufficiently just, or rigorous, or scientific, but because subordination to *any* law is a "yoke of bondage" (Galatians 5:1).

In the last analysis, the moralist's conception of perfection entails the enslavement of freedom. It is perfectly illustrated by the famous remark of Thomas Huxley, "If some great power would agree to make me always think what is true and do what is right, on condition of being turned a sort of clock and wound up every morning before I got out of bed, I should instantly close with the author."[4] In Huxley's heaven there would indeed be no "deviationists," but neither would there be any fun. It would be a kingdom of mechanical men whose freedom had been exchanged for reflexes perfectly conditioned to respond negatively to the stimulus of "naughty" and positively to that of "nice."

Such an existence could scarcely be called "living." If man really is a free agent, then a situation which stifled his freedom would more appropriately be called "death." St. Paul is therefore quite consistent in concluding that any "righteousness of works" is a veritable living death: "If there had been a law given which could *make alive*, verily righteousness would have been of the law" (Galatians 3:21). Or, in his more familiar words, "The letter killeth, but the spirit giveth life" (2 Corinthians 3:6). Or again, "For freedom did Christ set us free [from the law]" (Galatians 5:1).

It must be acknowledged, of course, that historically the Church has unfortunately often followed the example of the Galatians. It has often concentrated upon the letter at the expense of the spirit and emphasized external actions *for their own sake*, whether teetotaling, or contributions to charity, or regular church attendance. At a time when the so-called "personality sciences" are discovering how

[3]This point is made by the contemporary psychiatrist, Th. Bovet, in his *Die Angst Vor Dem Lebendigen Gott* (Bern: Verlag Paul Haupt, 1948), p. 63.
[4]Cited by Joseph Wood Krutch, op. cit., p. 60.

damaging rigid moralism can be, a "Christianity" which absolutized such petty observances would be derelict on two counts: Instead of recognizing in these sciences simply the experimental confirmation of biblical insight, it would be cast in the role of die-hard defender of an untenable moral code. And it would fail society in its hour of need. For although science does help to pry men loose from a strait-jacket morality, it also sets in motion the corrosion of all ethical standards. Such an emergency high-lights the uniqueness of the biblical alternative. It, too, transcends legalism, but without becoming cynical. It both avoids the abuses of rigorism and provides a heightened ethical incentive. The fulfillment of freedom, which both moralist and relativist are seeking, *agape* establishes in *fact*.

CHAPTER VII

SIN MISCONCEIVED AS INTRINSIC TO HUMAN NATURE

And God saw everything that he had made, and behold, it was very good.

—Genesis 1:31

In contrast to the rather optimistic belief that the individual can perfect himself by an effort of will, most of the world's philosophers and many of its artists have taken a radically different view. The majority subscribe to the melancholy doctrine that man's woes are due to the very "conditions of human existence" or to human nature as such. It is stated with unusual candor in the following account of a famous Buddhist's teaching:

By sin Nichiren understood nothing else than estrangement from the truth . . . the falling away of individuals from the primordial oneness of universal life. But sin was not merely a matter of the individual person, it was the common heritage of all beings. . . .[1]

This sophisticated teaching sometimes succeeds in infiltrating the popular mind itself. Naïve common sense is intimidated by the wholly arbitrary claim that any philosophy is superficial which lacks a "tragic sense of life"; in other words, that one must be pessimistic in order to be profound.

Before swallowing such a claim the man in the street may fairly ask for its credentials. On what grounds is all existence placed under blanket condemnation? A clue is provided by Plato's famous myth of the cave, which teaches that the everyday world is but a passing shadow of the true reality, which belongs to an immaterial, nontemporal sphere of being. For Plato, as for so many other thinkers, the "religious" problem is how the soul may escape from its bondage here below and return to the disembodied state whence it originally "fell." By what value judgment is this alleged realm exalted and the world of common sense disparaged? Plato's yardstick is the same one which underlies the "determinist's creed": the ideal of perfect "knowability," in the sense of absolute certainty. Knowledge in man's present state is always partial, never certain. Even the wisest and

[1]Masaharu Anesaki, *History of Japanese Religion* (London: Kegan Paul, Trench, Trubner, & Co., Ltd., 1930), p. 201.

oldest scientist knows only a fraction of what there is to know, and his surest knowledge attains no more than a high degree of probability. This is why the Oriental scoffs at the achievements of Western science as a chasing after wind.

The world of "true Being" which the philosopher postulates is custom-built to remedy these defects. Plato calls it a "colorless, formless, intangible essence, visible only to the mind, the pilot of the soul."[2] The soul's present state of exile is due to its failure to hold fast to the intellectual vision which it formerly enjoyed. Accordingly, the way of salvation consists in recollecting, by philosophical contemplation, this precious forgotten knowledge. The soul thereby slips its earth-bound moorings and soars back to its true home. Plato would have no difficulty in agreeing with the Buddhist that sin is "estrangement from the truth" and that salvation consists in "enlightenment." Both acknowledge the same ultimate standard of judgment: the good is conceived in terms of absolutely certain knowledge, while its opposite, evil, is merely ignorance.

THE INDICTMENT

Whoever thus deifies knowledge will discover all manner of grounds on which to convict the everyday world of obstructionism. In addition to his primary target, human freedom, he trains his fire on the mere fact of time, matter in general, the flesh in particular, and all desire whatever. These separate counts in the indictment will be considered in order.

Philosophers and poets throughout the ages have been nearly unanimous in their lament over man's involvement in the temporal process. It automatically precludes perfect knowledge, for the future is at best only imperfectly anticipated and the past only fragmentarily remembered. The realm of time is the realm of change, whereas the truth is that which never changes. As Plato declares, "That which is apprehended by intelligence and reason is always in the same state; but that which is conceived by opinion with the help of sensation and without reason is always in a process of becoming and perishing and never really is."[3] In this spirit the contemporary philosopher,

[2]*Phaedrus,* ※247.
[3]Plato, *Timaeus,* ※28.

W. T. Stace, declares that the "unifying vision" of truth must be timeless.[4] Hence temporal existence itself is a stigma.[5]

The poet is likewise afflicted with melancholy and yearning at the thought of being the prisoner of time. The spectre of everything being swallowed up by its insatiable ravages drives him to exclaim with T. S. Eliot, "To be conscious is not to be in time."[6] Nearly every poet has composed at least one stanza on the sadness of transient existence. None surpasses "Tomorrow and tomorrow and tomorrow creeps in this petty pace from day to day until the last syllable of recorded time."

Next in the indictment comes matter, the mere fact of there being physical objects. It is an opaque, inert, intractable stuff, impenetrable to the pure intellectual vision. Moreover, whereas the intellect thirsts for the "primordial oneness of universal life," matter is the seat of multiplicity and diversity. As the hated "principle of individuation," it splits reality into myriad fragments. The philosophy of Schopenhauer is almost obsessed with this refrain, although it neither originates nor ends with him. W. T. Stace expresses the incompatibility of material existence with perfect knowledge by describing the latter as an experience in which

all distinctions between one thing and another . . . self and notself, are abolished, overcome, transcended, so that all the *different* things in the world become *one*, become identical with one another.[7]

When applied to the individual, this attitude entails the disparagement of his bodily nature. The Hindu lying on his bed of nails is simply putting into practice a doctrine of contempt for the body and mortification of the flesh. He gives concrete expression to the maxim so popular among the Greeks, "The body is a tomb." Its worst offense is that, by means of the five senses, it attracts the mind to the world of temporal and physical objects, thereby plunging it deeper into ignorance and illusion. Moreover, it subjects reason to the caprices of the biological organism and limits its perspective to a particular locus in space and time. Aristotle only echoes Greek

[4]W. T. Stace, *Religion and the Modern Mind* (New York: J. B. Lippincott Co., 1952), pp. 231, 238.

[5]For a classic statement of this position, see Plotinus, *Enneads*, III, 7, 11.

[6]T. S. Eliot, *Four Quartets* (London: Faber and Faber, 1944), p. 10.

[7]W. T. Stace, op. cit., p. 230. Like other mystics, the author also holds reason responsible for the fragmentation of primordial oneness.

thought in general when he complains that man's rational nature is impeded by the exercise of bodily functions.[8]

The man for whom complete knowledge is the ultimate goal also resents "the flesh" on the ground that it is the seat of desire. For two reasons he finds desire "undesirable." First, it destroys his precious self-sufficiency. The thirst for knowledge for its own sake always goes hand in hand with the craving for self-sufficiency and indeed often turns out to be simply the means to this end. Desire, by relating a man to something outside himself, makes his happiness dependent upon circumstances beyond his control. Second, desire is incompatible with the idolization of knowledge as the supreme good. By preventing the knower from being completely "disinterested," it introduces a "subjective" factor to distort the clarity of intellectual apprehension.

The campaign against the flesh frequently centers on the sex impulse. The pagan esteem for celibacy per se, so remote from the over-all biblical outlook, scarcely requires documentation. What does require emphasis is the fact that prudery in such matters is no part of biblical Christianity, even if Christians themselves have not always realized this.

CHRISTIAN THINKING SUBVERTED

Christian thinking has been so successfully infiltrated by pagan value judgments that most people simply take it for granted that Christianity has a negative view of the world in general and a repressive attitude toward the flesh in particular. They can certainly point to numerous historical illustrations in their support. The medieval Church provides ammunition by contrasting the divine or "eternal" order with the merely "temporal." From the hermits of the Egyptian desert to the austerities of the Puritans, Christians have imagined that full devotion to God demanded the renunciation of his world. Of all such advocates of physical austerities none is fiercer than St. Jerome, whose writings bristle with passages like the following, in which he describes the ideal Christian life as he conceives it:

I dwelt in the desert, in the vast solitude which gives the hermit his savage home, parched by the burning sun. . . . Sackcloth disfigured my unshapely limbs, and my skin from long neglect became as black as the

[8]Aristotle, *Nicomachean Ethics*, Book I, Chapter 13, line 30.

Ethiopian's. Tears and groans were everyday my portion; if drowsiness
chanced to overcome my struggles against it, my bare bones, which hardly
held together, clashed against the ground. Of my food and drink I say
nothing: for even in sickness the solitaries have nothing but cold water,
and to eat one's food cooked is looked upon as self-indulgence. . . . My
face was pale and my frame chilled with fasting. . . . I do not blush to
avow my abject misery; rather I lament that I am not now as then I was.[9]

This negative attitude toward the self and the world has at times
managed to become part and parcel of the definition of sainthood.
In the words of a recent student of medieval saints, "The foundation,
the root, of the love of self is the desire of things, that fatal wanting
which St. Francis all his life proclaims to be so deadly, and À Kempis,
like St. Francis, insists that desire must be rooted out altogether if
perfection is to be attained."[10]

This is simply another illustration of how easily a saintly but uncritical mind may be betrayed into a thoroughly pagan outlook.
Rightly perceiving that some desires are "bad," he may wrongly
conclude that the fault lies in the nature of desire itself. Unable by
solitary effort to accomplish its purification, and neglecting to ask
God for its transformation, he may clamor instead for its extinction.
Whenever a Christian takes this position, his thinking has jumped
the track. It has in fact, if not in intent, gone into the service of
another, very different religion.

Christian theology, instead of providing solid ground from which
to criticize these ascetic tendencies, has often provided them with a
persuasive defense. Thomas Aquinas, for example, when he arranges
matter on the lower half of his scale of realities, bifurcates human
nature in the familiar dichotomy of mind and matter, thereby sacri-
ficing biblical anthropology to Aristotelian. His Roman Catholic followers make a brave effort to say that, although "mind is better,"
matter is still "good." In practice, however, the consequences of

[9]Epistle 22, 7. Cited by Kenneth E. Kirk, *The Vision of God* (London: Longmans, Green, & Co., 1932), p. 176.
[10]Gamaliel Bradford, op. cit., p. 120. The author cites to similar effect a quotation from the Spanish thinker, Molinos: "The soul must find itself dead to its
will, desire, endeavor, understanding, and thought; willing as if it did not will;
desiring as if it did not desire; understanding as if it did not understand; thinking
as if it did not think; without inclination to anything, embracing equally contempt and honors, benefits and corrections. Oh what a happy soul is that which
is thus dead and annihilated! It lives no longer in itself, because God lives in it."
P. 141.

choosing this "lesser good" are just as unpleasant as if it were "bad." Accordingly, the saint turns his back upon this "lower" order.

For the two-story edifice of St. Thomas, Protestant orthodoxy often substitutes two intersecting "dimensions." This device does have the merit of making explicit the ultimate irreconcilability of the "lower" and "higher" realms of being in Aquinas's system. At bottom, however, this Protestant alternative is no improvement, for, despite protests to the contrary, it in fact is obliged to fall back upon the dualism of mind and body as the paradigm of the relation between the divine and the human. Although it has the technical merit of adhering to this dualism more rigorously than the Thomists, it thereby ends in a less biblical position than Roman Catholicism. For the inconsistencies of Thomism, which no amount of dialectical cleverness can conceal, are often committed for the sake of a more biblical conception of the relation between God and man.

In our own day Nicolas Berdyaev makes the blanket assertion that the temporal and spatial world is the source of all the misfortunes of man.[11] Another example is Paul Tillich, who declares that creation coincides with the fall.[12] Although he is careful not to say that creation *is* the fall, he fails to draw any distinction between them. A biblical theology would at all costs avoid the slightest possibility of ambiguity or misunderstanding on this score. It would make clear that nothing intrinsic to creation anticipates a fall.

These embarrassments will continue to beset Christian thinking until it develops explicitly the philosophical implications of the Bible, instead of casting about for a ready-made metaphysical framework upon which to hang a few biblical adornments. Such philosophies always turn out to be a Procrustean bed on which biblical Christianity is disfigured.

FATAL CONSEQUENCES

If the highest good is unshakable certainty, and if this goal is incompatible with the conditions of spatiotemporal existence, then a man's consequent attitude toward human life will be one of uncompromising hostility. He will define the good as the very opposite of anything in human experience. This is the famous *via negativa* of

[11]See Nicolas Berdyaev, *The Divine and the Human* (London: Geoffrey Bles, 1949), Chapter 14.
[12]Paul Tillich, *Systematic Theology*, Vol. I (University of Chicago Press, 1951), pp. 255f.

the mystic, whether Eastern or Western. As one writer has eloquently put it:

If, he [the mystic] argues, God is the contradiction of our human faculties in the sense that the one is exclusive of the other, then by contradicting, or negating, these same faculties we make ourselves like Him, so as to attain knowledge of Him, even oneness with Him. . . . What little our human faculties can discern on the path is of no avail to purge the spiritual eye of the humours of this world in order that it may behold the gleams of inspiration which flash upon it now and then: it must be closed in voluntary blindness. I have not exaggerated. This, and nothing less than this, is the secret of what St. John of the Cross means by describing the pilgrimage to eternity as the Dark Night of the Soul.[13]

A man who defines the good as the very opposite of anything in human experience will often take pride in his contempt for life. His animus against this world becomes the measure of his devotion to the other. The present writer once had a conversation with a woman who had been a friend of one of the most notorious Nazi brutes. "He was a fine man," she said; "he should have been a priest."

"A priest?" was the surprised reply.

"Yes. He was such an idealist."

"An idealist? How do you mean?"

"Oh, he hated the world so."

However astonishing at first glance, this equation of idealism with hatred of the world follows with inexorable logic from the deification of noetic certainty. Some Western philosophers have been deterred by a healthy common sense from pressing their logic so far. Some have even advocated taking a responsible role in society. However "admirable" this sense of duty, the Eastern sage has no trouble in pointing out its inconsistency. Plato's wise man returns to the cave, not because of his logic, but in spite of it. This self-contradiction runs through most idealistic philosophy. It may reflect credit upon the thinker's sense of social responsibility but not upon the coherence of his thought.[14]

Oriental philosophers have had better logic and fewer scruples. The ultimate issue of the common ideal which they share with their Western counterparts has been expressed in stark candor by a Sufi mystic:

[13]Paul E. More, *Christian Mysticism* (London: S.P.C.K., 1932), pp. 59f. Any similarity between this theology and that of Karl Barth is hardly coincidental.
[14]This point is beautifully made by Arthur O. Lovejoy in his *The Great Chain of Being* (Cambridge, Mass.: Harvard University Press, 1948), p. 39.

"Thine existence is a sin with which no other sin can be compared."[15] If, when stated in such a straightforward way, this teaching sounds fantastic to Western ears, this is due to a residual biblical heritage. Before assuming that "It cannot happen here," however, one would do well to look beneath the surface of European culture. In its Graeco-Roman phase, as noted in a previous chapter, there were numerous echoes of the Homeric dictum, "Better never to have been born at all." Although the advent of Christianity forced this value judgment partly underground, it has never ceased to reassert itself and, with the waning of Christian influence, has begun to emerge again in pagan nakedness. A contemporary philosopher believes that "all beings are infected by the same disease, the disease of existence."[16]

In the world of literature and the arts, especially, a creeping *taedium vitae* has made considerable inroads upon the modern mind. The recurrence of the themes of "alienation" and "estrangement" in contemporary literature has been prematurely interpreted by some Christian commentators as a rediscovery on the "secular" plane of basic Christian categories. The sense in which Christianity speaks of estrangement, however, is that of a violated relation of personal trust between men and God, whereas the sense in which most modern authors use it is precisely that of the Buddhist: it is, as a review in the *New Yorker* magazine puts it, "the entrapment of the spirit in the flesh, and the shadow cast by eternity upon time."[17]

The abhorrence of human existence as such has an ancient lineage in Western literature. Denis de Rougemont, in his remarkable study *Passion and Society*, traces it to its origin in pagan religion. The Italian poet Giacomo Leopardi expresses it as well as any:

All that exists is evil . . . everything exists only to achieve evil, existence itself is an evil. . . . There is no other good than non-existence.[18]

The final step in the argument is taken by the Spanish poet Calderón when he says, "The greatest crime of man is that he ever was born."

[15]Quoted by George F. Moore, *History of Religions* (New York: Charles Scribner's Sons, Vol. 2, 1919), p. 442.
[16]W. T. Stace, *Time and Eternity* (Princeton University Press, 1952), p. 95.
[17]The *New Yorker* magazine, Sept. 4, 1954, p. 75.
[18]Iris Origo, *Leopardi: A Study In Solitude* (British Book Centre, 1954). Quoted in *Time* magazine, Aug. 2, 1954, p. 78.

With this kind of ancestry it is not surprising that contemporary art and literature is characterized, as Lionel Trilling notes, by " 'a real loathing of living forms and living beings' . . . a disgust with history and society and the state."[19]

The crude manifestations of this *contemptus mundi* to which our generation is growing accustomed are anticipated by the more refined sentiments of Henry James on the death of his beloved. He writes that she now lived

as a steady unfaltering luminary in the mind rather than as a flickering wasting earth-stifled lamp. . . . The more I think of her the more perfectly satisfied I am to have her translated from this changing realm of fact to the steady realm of thought.[20]

This last remark is an appropriate reminder that hatred of the world is dictated by the ideal of perfect "knowability."

An even more explicit statement of the same attitude is made by Robert Louis Stevenson:

This stuff [matter], when not purified by the lustration of fire, rots uncleanly into something we call life; seized through all its atoms with a pediculous malady; swelling with tumors which become independent, sometimes even (by a horrid prodigy) locomotory . . . And to put the last touch on this mountain mass of the revolting and the inconceivable, all these prey upon each other . . . What a monstrous spectre is this man, the disease of the agglutinated dust.[21]

Among the countless illustrations that could be cited from the mid-twentieth century, Robinson Jeffers's poem "Inscription for a Gravestone" declares unmistakably that death is preferable to life, chiefly for the reason that it constitutes escape from the body and is beyond the "fictions called good and evil."[22] Sherwood Anderson says it more prosaically:

As for the end, I have often thought that when it comes, there will be a kind of real comfort in the fact that the self will go then. There is some

[19]Lionel Trilling, *The Liberal Imagination* (New York: Doubleday Anchor Books, 1953), p. 254. The author is quoting Ortega.
[20]Leon Edel, *Henry James: The Untried Years* (New York: J. B. Lippincott Co., 1953), p. 325.
[21]*The Works of Robert Louis Stevenson* (Boston: The Jefferson Press, n.d.), Vol. 2, pp. 595f. Cited by D. R. G. Owen, *Scientism, Man, and Religion* (Philadelphia: The Westminster Press, 1952), pp. 162f.
[22]See "Inscription for a Gravestone" in *The Selected Poetry of Robinson Jeffers* (New York: Random House, 1937), p. 480.

kind of universal thing we will pass into that will in any event give us escape from this disease of self.[23]

The attempt is sometimes made to silence critical discussion of these and similar utterances by means of the claim that they merely "give voice to the underlying reality of our present situation" or that they "speak to our condition." Actually such literature represents not so much an unbiased examination of the human situation as an attempt to influence it. Harry and Bonaro Overstreet make the following remarks about writers of this kind:

They are avid gleaners of catastrophic news—and since they lack the power to feel drama in the things that are going on normally and well within our nation and the world, their disproportionate and insistent stress upon what is going wrong tends to cast a weird, apocalyptic light over the human scene at the very time when we are most needing to see it in the light of creative rationality.[24]

The unwary reader is sometimes disarmed by the claim that a poet is by definition a seer whose transcendent message may not be questioned. This is an ingenious way of demanding immunity to criticism. The privilege of seeking converts to a particular religion entails the obligation to label one's efforts as such.

Lionel Trilling has exposed a subtle connection between the cult of catastrophe and the contempt of self. He who despises himself, writes Professor Trilling, may gain a hypnotic power over all who will believe his fatalistic utterances:

The sense of evil is properly managed only when it is not allowed to be preponderant over the sense of self . . . we have to ask ourselves whether our quick antagonism to [the] mild recognition of pleasure does not imply an impatience with the self, a degree of yielding to what Hannah Arendt calls the irresistible temptation of disintegration, of identification by submission to the grandeur of historical necessity which is so much more powerful than the self. It is possible that our easily expressed contempt for the smiling aspects [of life] and our covert impulse to yield to the historical process are a way of acquiring charism . . . which, in the sociopolitical context, is the quality of power and leadership that seems to derive from a direct connection with great supernatural forces. . . . It is that peculiar charism which has always been inherent in death.[25]

The field of art and literature is not the only one in which the modern temper reveals a certain animus against human existence.

[23]Quoted in the New York *Herald Tribune Book Review*, April 12, 1953.
[24]Harry and Bonaro Overstreet, op. cit., p. 101.
[25]Lionel Trilling, *The Opposing Self* (New York: The Viking Press, 1955), pp. 99–102.

It is implied, as noted in an earlier chapter, by the undue exaltation of the scientific method. The scientist who applies it to areas beyond its competence, the description of fact and the explanation of un-free acts and occurrences, is continually frustrated. A personal factor inevitably intrudes upon every controlled experiment. In a value system which regards knowledge as the supreme good, this residual "subjective element" will be resented as the worm in the apple. Though not always consistently or even directly expressed, this anti-personal bias works behind the scenes in a good deal of scientific literature. As Joseph Wood Krutch has so prophetically observed, when it does make its appearance, it wears a tragic mask. Its ulti-mate outcome would be human sacrifice, not indeed to an idol of wood or stone, but on the altar of "impersonal truth"—or even a heartless vegetable from Mars.

The recrudescence of the pagan contempt for human life is also evident in contemporary philosophy, particularly existentialism. One of its principal spokesmen, Martin Heidegger, regards human exist-ence as shot through with the stigma of "nothingness," a situation which can only be overcome in death. Especially significant is the fact that Heidegger explicitly designates this condition as "guilt." A human being is "guilty" by definition! There could be no more perfect illustration of the conception of "sin" as intrinsic to human nature or of the devaluation of man that follows from it. Since man is guilty through his very existence, the only difference is between those who acknowledge and accept this fact and those who do not. The criterion by which the sheep are separated from the goats has not changed. It is still knowledge. Although the "absolute knowl-edge" to which the mystic aspires is now regarded as impossible, there still remains the aristocracy of those who realize how utterly repulsive man's condition is.

This attitude is beautifully illustrated by Robert Penn Warren in his *Brother to Dragons*. He maintains that "there is no forgiveness for our being human. It is the inexpugnable error." However, since he also holds the concomitant view that "all is redeemed in knowledge," one would expect him to find salvation in the mere awareness that existence is itself a sin. It is therefore no surprise that he further de-clares, "The recognition of complicity is the beginning of inno-cence."[26] If self-incrimination is the road to innocence, then the most

[26]Robert Penn Warren, *Brother to Dragons* (New York: Random House, 1953), pp. 24, 195, 214.

innocent are those who castigate themselves most fiercely. This verbal jugglery would be comic if it did not provide such a plausible excuse for inculpating one's neighbor as well. By insisting upon his guilt one does him the dubious service of establishing his innocence.

T. S. Eliot carries this logic one step further when he declares, "Our only health is the disease . . . To be restored, our sickness must grow worse."[27] This reasoning is responsible for the existentialist's perverse gratification in dwelling on the nauseating character of existence, a pastime not so new as he may imagine. Walter Pater, referring to ancient Rome, detects

that species of almost insane preoccupation with the materialities of our mouldering flesh, that luxury of disgust in gazing on corruption.[28]

According to Heidegger, human life is a mad roller coaster which will end in death. Like the oriental mystic, he holds out as the supreme goal simply the act of dying in the right way. Man, he says, acquires a superpower from hurling himself into death.[29] This is the twentieth-century outgrowth of Socrates's remark that philosophy is the study of death.[30] And this statement, in turn, only makes explicit the implication of Aristotle's observation that the philosopher's goal of "pure, unalloyed thinking" is possible, not by virtue of what is human in man, but what is "divine."[31]

Contempt and disgust with human life is also one of the main themes of another contemporary existentialist, Jean Paul Sartre. The mood of his writing can be gathered from the following quotation from one of his novels:

There is a white hole in the wall, a mirror. It is a trap. I know I am going to let myself be caught in it. I have. The grey thing appears in the mirror. I go over and look at it, I can no longer get away.

It is the reflection of my face . . .

My glance slowly and wearily travels over my forehead, my cheeks: it finds nothing firm, it is stranded. Obviously there are a nose, two eyes, and a mouth, but none of it makes sense, there is not even a human expression. . . . What I see is well below the monkey, on the fringe of the vegetable world, on the level of the jellyfish. . . . I see the insipid flesh blossoming

[27]T. S. Eliot, op. cit., pp. 20f.

[28]Walter Pater, *Marius, the Epicurean* (New York: Modern Library, Random House, n.d.), p. 49. The words are those of Théophile Gautier.

[29]Martin Heidegger, *Sein Und Zeit* (Tübingen: Neomarius Verlag, 1949), p. 384.

[30]Plato, *Phaedo*, paragraph 81.

[31]Aristotle, *Nicomachean Ethics*, Book 10, Chapter 7, lines 26–28.

and palpitating with abandon. The eyes especially are horrible seen so close. They are glassy, soft, blind, red-rimmed, they look like fish scales.[32]

Sentiments like these have moved Gabriel Marcel to characterize existentialism as an elaborate technique for the "vilification of man."

Sartre has tried to extricate himself from the plain implications of his philosophy by declaring that existentialism is really a kind of humanism. The attempt, however, is a transparent failure. It stands as a sober warning to every humanist to take a second look at his bedfellows. The cultural achievements to which he points with such pride, and upon which he bases his confidence toward the future, are precisely the area in which man's ancient enemy has established a bridgehead. The "lofty expressions of the human spirit," in art, literature, science, and philosophy, have all too frequently denied human responsibility, resented the "personal factor" as an impediment to knowledge, and, consequently, entailed a proud contempt for human existence. In so doing they have become accomplices, intentional or not, in the vilification of man.

CONTRAST WITH THE BIBLE

There is no more striking contrast to this baleful world-weariness than the first chapter of Genesis, where the events of creation are accompanied by the refrain, "And God saw that it was good." Christian thinking sometimes tends to abandon this evaluation and to slip over into the pagan outlook when it deals with the fact of time. The Bible has simply never heard that time, as distinct from many of the things that happen *in* time, is something to be redeemed *from*. When it speaks of the ultimate fulfillment, it uses definitely temporal terms: "life everlasting," "world without end." The phrase "eternal life" means, in the original Greek, not a timeless state but "the life of the age to come." The recent book by Oscar Cullmann, *Christ and Time*,[33] demonstrates conclusively that the Bible evaluates no state higher than the temporal.

Genuinely distressed by the terrible things that do happen in time, the philosopher generally takes the only alternative available to the man who reckons without a Redeemer. He throws the baby out with

[32]Jean Paul Sartre, *Nausea*, translated by Lloyd Alexander (London: A New Directions book, 1949), pp. 27f.
[33]Oscar Cullmann, *Christ and Time*, translated by Floyd V. Filson (London: SCM Press, Ltd., 1951).

the bath. Better no time at all, he concludes, than the tragedies of history. Even in philosophy, however, one neglects God at one's peril. The philosopher is betrayed into an impossible intellectual position. Without time there can be no activity and no life. A timeless state is a static one. The Bible therefore asks those who would be rid of time, "Are you willing to exchange the temporal condition for a lifeless and static one?" The reply to this question is regularly equivocal. The man who cannot endure temporal existence also finds difficulty in coming to terms with a completely nontemporal state. He consequently falls back on phrases of highly dubious meaning, such as "timeless activity" or "an eternity which is not without life."[34] The resort to ambiguity in the face of a philosophical embarrassment is a device as old as philosophy itself. But unless one can convince oneself that obscurity is an intellectual asset the Bible certainly is in the stronger philosophical position.

The biblical affirmation of the goodness of matter is also unequivocal. As Archbishop Temple puts it, Christianity is "the most avowedly materialist of all the great religions."[35] Hence it has no embarrassment about describing heaven in materialistic terms or insisting upon the resurrection of the body. Whoever rejects this imagery on the ground that it is "crude" does well to recall that the only alternative is a pagan devaluation of the world. Without a body there is simply no self at all. In this, as in everything, Christianity is an all-or-nothing proposition. It wants no part of a heaven inhabited by ectoplasmic phantoms. This issue is raised explicitly by St. Luke:

Handle me, and see. For a spirit hath not flesh and bones, as ye see me have. And when he had thus spoken, he showed them his hands and his feet. And while they yet believed not for joy, and wondered, he said unto them, Have ye here any meat? And they gave him a piece of a broiled fish, and of an honeycomb. And he took it, and did eat before them. (Luke 24:39-43.)

[34] An example of the theologian's embarrassment in trying to talk about an "eternity" which is neither temporal nor static is Paul Tillich's *Systematic Theology*, Vol. 1, pp, 256-58 and 276-78. John Marsh, in his book, *The Fullness of Time* (New York: Harper & Brothers, 1952), attempts to refute the contention of Cullmann that eternity as the Bible conceives it is time without end. But Marsh falls into exactly the same difficulty. He is unwilling to grant either that eternity is temporal or that it is static.

[35] William Temple, *Nature, Man, and God* (London: The Macmillan Company, 1935), p. 478.

The crowning testimony to the goodness of matter in general, and specifically of the human body, is, of course, the incarnation. If this momentous fact is true, it entails a metaphysical position unique in the history of thought. The doctrine of the incarnation declares seriously, and not just "mythologically," that the difference between man and God is not primarily spatial, temporal, or physical. Though it wisely leaves open the question of whether God has a body, it does affirm that his nature is not incompatible with corporeal existence.

The biblical attitude toward desire is similar. The fact that some desires are destructive does not dictate the extinction of all desire as such. Here again the Bible enjoys an intellectual advantage. One cannot suppress desire without *desiring* to do so. The philosophy which prescribes its systematic annihilation is thus in contradiction with itself. Desire in some form is constitutive of human nature. No man can undertake a campaign against it without having first presupposed it. On strictly intellectual grounds the biblical view is stronger.

An indirect corroboration of this is the fact that in India, where asceticism is carried to its extreme, there exist side by side with it orgiastic practices which can only be described in language unprintable in this country. The history of medieval monasticism is likewise notable for its seamy side, and the private lives of many of the famous mystics are also a carefully guarded secret.

The biblical answer to the problem raised by unruly desires is characteristically positive: their transformation into constructive ones by the concrete agency of God. The Bible, for example, is never content simply to repress and negate sex or any other natural capacity simply because it can be abused. Such an attitude would impugn both the goodness and the power of God. It would imply that he was wrong to endow men with sex and unable to reclaim it from perversion. Although abstinence may be preferred to wrongdoing, in itself it is not meritorious in the least. It only conceals the real problem. The Bible, on the contrary, is never content to side-step an obstacle. It will settle for nothing less than complete victory. Its God wants, not the annihilation of unruly passions, but their conversion, for the greatest powers for evil may also be transformed into even greater forces for good. Sex, in particular, though the source of very great evils, can also become a unique medium for the perfect expression of *agape*. To stifle it simply in order to prevent its abuse would be to cut off one's nose to spite one's face. In short, the biblical answer to the misuse of any natural faculty is not *disuse* but redemption.

This is the basis for the biblical reply to the complaint that desire in any form constitutes a subjective factor which precludes perfect knowledge. While granting that a man's thinking may be distorted by wayward desires, the Bible also, and perhaps more consistently, holds the converse. It declares that knowledge is only made perfect by the "right" desires. True understanding is achieved, not at the expense of the heart, but as a consequence of its reorientation. Hence, "the fear of the Lord is the beginning of wisdom." Or, in the more eloquent words in which St. Paul quotes Isaiah:

Hearing ye shall hear, and shall not understand; and seeing ye shall see, and not perceive. For the *heart* of this people is waxed gross, and their ears are dull of hearing, and their eyes have they closed; lest they should see with their eyes, and hear with their ears, and understand with their heart, and should be converted, and I should heal them (Acts 28:26–27).

For the Bible, creation is good because of who created it. The watershed which separates this view from pessimistic philosophies and religions reflects the difference between their respective gods. When knowledge, conceived in terms of immediate or demonstrable certainty, is deified, the derogation of the world follows. For the Bible, on the contrary, knowledge, though a very great good, is not an end in itself, and indeed is only made perfect when devoted to the right end, the service of *agape*. Without love, it runs amuck. In St. Paul's words, "If I understand all mysteries and all knowledge . . . but have not love, I am nothing." (1 Corinthians 12:2).

NOTE

The attitude of St. Paul toward "the flesh," so often invoked in defense of Christian asceticism, has been the subject of much illuminating research. The gist of the most recent scholarship on the subject is that he employs the term "flesh" in a highly technical sense, derived from Hebraic rather than Greek usage, and signifying any area of life which is subjected to a false god. For an excellent analysis, see J. A. T. Robinson, *The Body* (Chicago: Henry Regnery Company, 1952).

St. Paul's attitude toward marriage is somewhat less clear. Of the few passages (chiefly in 1 Corinthians 7) which suggest a negative view, most can be accounted for as *ad hoc* recommendations to meet a specific local situation rather than general principles. Some are undoubtedly influenced by the notorious promiscuity of the Corinthians, while others are due to the expectation that Christ would return at any moment.

Less easy to explain, however, is the following statement:

He that is unmarried is careful for the things of the Lord, how he may please the Lord. But he that is married is careful for the things of the world, how he may please his wife, and is divided (1 Corinthians 7:32–34).

Rather than try to extenuate St. Paul for this remark, it seems simpler to recall that the Bible contains within itself its own internal principles of self-criticism, against which this and other unguarded remarks of St. Paul can be tested. The above statement, when so judged, is less true to the spirit of the Bible as a whole than is the following, contrary statement, also by St. Paul:

Am I not free? Am I not an apostle? . . . Have we [Paul and Barnabas] no right to lead about a wife who is a believer, even as the rest of the apostles, and the brethren of the Lord, and Peter? (2 Corinthians 9:1,5.)

Derrick S. Bailey's *The Mystery of Love and Marriage*, despite its neoplatonic leanings, expresses truly and unequivocally the Christian conception of the sacredness of sex and marriage (New York: Harper and Brothers, 1952).

CHAPTER VIII

ST. AUGUSTINE'S ACHIEVEMENTS AND MISTAKES

Prove all things; hold fast that which is good.
—1 Thessalonians 5:21

The two principal alternatives to the biblical view of sin have been described: the simple moralism which conceives sin as the mere breaking of taboos, and the ubiquitous doctrine, especially among philosophers and aesthetes, that the mere fact of human existence itself constitutes an intolerable stigma. Each view is the product of an attempt to fit the facts of idolatry into a framework prescribed by pagan categories. Though neither can thoroughly digest these facts, each retains a garbled fragment of the truth. The first appreciates the necessity for some objective reference in the exercise of freedom, though conceiving it statically, in terms of law. The second understands that sin is prior to individual acts of choice, but traces it to a defective human nature rather than to misplaced allegiance.

Unfortunately Christian thought has not sufficiently distinguished the biblical from these two pagan views, but instead has often confused it with one or the other. On two historic occasions the Church was rocked to its foundations by disputes over the nature of sin. In their struggle against Pelagius and against late medieval Catholicism, respectively, St. Augustine and the Reformers formulated for all time and in unmistakable terms Christianity's case against moralism. The tragedy, however, was that in doing so they fell into the opposite error. They did not consistently oppose moralism with a biblical view of sin but lapsed instead into a disparagement of human nature.

They thus provide a classic illustration of how controversy perpetuates itself. One party first discerns a conspicuous error in the other's thinking. Aware that fallacious theory gives rise to destructive practice, he feels obliged to assail it with all his might. No one, however, can confine himself merely to negative criticism. Every criticism implies a positive affirmation (excepting only the case of purely formal logic). The philosopher or theologian cannot object to his opponent's position without saying why. And the moment he states his reason he willy-nilly endorses an alternative answer to the question at issue. He may not be aware of this; he may even disclaim any positive view whatever. But this only means that he takes to himself a bedfellow whose credentials he has not examined.[1] Any inadequacy in his unconscious premise is sure to be exploited by his opponent. A vicious circle thus begins in which each side is right in what it negates but wrong in what it affirms. Each sees the other's error so clearly that he can attribute it only to willful blindness. What began as a serious discussion of a live issue degenerates into a treadmill of mutual recrimination. This is what happened in the debate between St. Augustine and Pelagius. As will be shown subsequently, the biblical alternative can combine the strength and avoid the weakness of each side.

The situation of St. Augustine, and also of the two principal Reformers, is not unlike that of the Western Allies in World War II. In desperation to defeat a manifest evil, they did not ask too many questions of their comrades in arms. So also the historic opponents of moralism. They concentrated so exclusively on the job at hand, the demolition of the belief in "sanctification by works," that they were not too particular about their intellectual alliances. Their victory was achieved with the help of a doctrine which is quite as alien to the biblical outlook as the ones which they overcame: the view that sin is intrinsic to human nature. They thereby bequeathed to future generations the still unfinished task of winning the peace.

THE CHURCH'S INDEBTEDNESS TO ST. AUGUSTINE

St. Augustine rendered the Church an invaluable service by exposing the dangers which lay hidden in the persuasive arguments of Pelagius. Not until Luther's time did anyone again so fully appreciate or so eloquently expound the pitfalls in a legalistic conception of sin. He brings to bear all the biblical arguments against it. He pointed out the lovelessness of a scheme in which each individual concentrates on establishing his own perfection. He was quick to discern the demon of self-righteousness and spiritual pride waiting at the top of the ladder of moral achievement.[2] He saw that a definition of righteousness in terms of what the individual could do for himself

[1]A prime example is the theology of Karl Barth. By steadfastly refusing to acknowledge the positive implications of his far-flung negations, he unwittingly allies himself with a metaphysic that is far more neoplatonic than Christian.

[2]The metaphor is Archbishop Temple's. See his *Basic Convictions* (New York: Harper & Brothers, 1936), p. 50.

diverts attention from that aspect of his behavior which is beyond his immediate control: his motives. And to disregard motives, of course, is to miss the entire point of the moral problem. If the sole criterion of conduct were mere external correctness, we could all become paragons of virtue simply by putting our minds to it. This prospect of an easy sainthood accounts for the perennial appeal of Pelagianism. It also explains why the moralist is driven by his very moral ardor to become the agent of evil. For to exempt a man's motives from judgment is to throw the door wide open to hypocrisy. If the motives behind his "good works" are tinged with resentment, envy, or moral competitiveness, his crusade against evil will only result in the poisoning of human relations. Unknown to himself, he has become an agent of the devil's fifth column. And finally, Augustine argues that, if man by his own good works could pile up sufficient merit to establish a claim against God, then it would be man who called the tune. The Almighty would be relegated to the role of a mere means to man's beatitude.

The Church will always be indebted to St. Augustine for the insight and the zeal with which he exposed these errors. This does not mean, however, that his counteraffirmations are beyond criticism.[3] Throughout his thought two incompatible strands are inextricably interwoven. The first is the view of sin as intrinsic to human nature and, second, a genuinely biblical train of thought. This involves him in inconsistency and thereby reduces his philosophical effectiveness, but it also helps to redeem him personally from some of the unfortunate implications of his doctrines. The following pages give an account of some of the unhappy measures by which he sought to refute Pelagius and of their continuing influence on some Protestant theology. These criticisms themselves, however, are heavily dependent upon the "happy inconsistencies" which impart to Augustine's thought a leaven of health not always present in that of his successors.

SIN MADE INTRINSIC

In search of a bulwark against the self-righteousness of Pelagius's moral giant, Augustine took refuge in the famous doctrine of original sin (*originale peccatum*). Entirely absent from the Bible, and sig-

[3]Not all of Augustine's errors can be explained as due simply to the exigencies of controversy. The main outline of his position was already clearly stated in his

nificantly rare in pre-Augustinian writings, this phrase owes its currency among the theologians of Western Christendom almost entirely to Augustine. (The Eastern Church, suspecting from the start that neither Augustine nor Pelagius had successfully stated the true Christian position, never committed itself to either side of the dispute.) Modern reinterpretations of it, notably that of Reinhold Niebuhr, have gone far toward ridding it of some of the objectionable connotations which it has acquired in popular thinking. Responsibility for these connotations, however, must be laid at the door of Augustine himself. He expressly held that, as a result of Adam's first sin, the entire human race was a "lump of perdition" (*massa perditionis*), standing under a double curse. By a so-called "seminal identity" with Adam it inherited a full share of his immeasurable guilt (*reatus*), though it had no part in his original transgression. By the process of generation each individual was infected with unruly and inordinate passion (*concupiscentia*) which both confirmed his guilt and at the same time constituted a partial punishment:

> Then, after his sin, he [Adam] was given into exile, and by his sin the whole race of which he was the root was corrupted in him, and thereby subjected to the penalty of death. And so it happened that all descended from him, and from the woman who had led him into sin, and was condemned at the same time with him—being the offspring of carnal lust on which the same punishment of disobedience was visited—were tainted with the original sin, and were by it drawn through divers errors and sufferings into that last and endless punishment which they suffer in common with the fallen angels. . . .
>
> Thus, then, matters stood. The whole mass of the human race was under condemnation, and was lying steeped and wallowing in misery, and was being tossed from one form of evil to another, and . . . was paying the well-merited penalty of that impious rebellion.[4]

In the later Middle Ages Augustine's version of original sin was gradually modified. Although the Roman Catholic Church never endorsed Pelagianism as a theory, and in fact continues to uphold the doctrine of original guilt, it did not develop a third alternative to the Augustine-Pelagius dilemma, but settled down into the "semi-Pelagianism" which it holds to the present day. By the time of the Protestant Reformation its practice had succumbed to many of the

---

De Diversis Quaestionibus ad Simplicianum, written some years before he had ever heard of Pelagius. See Norman P. Williams, *The Ideas of the Fall and of Original Sin* (London: Longmans, Green & Co., Ltd., 1927), pp. 326–35.
[4]St. Augustine, *Enchiridion*, Chapters 26 and 27.

abuses against which Augustine had fought. The subtleties of scholastic speculation, which in theory might skate around Pelagianism, had not prevented its recrudescence in the everyday usage of the Church. The system of penance and indulgences had tended to make salvation a thing for sale and virtue a matter of almsgiving and telling beads. The symbol of this attitude was the treasury of merit. The theory was that the saints, by their excessive good works, had accumulated more merits than the minimum necessary for salvation. Under the auspices of the Church, withdrawals could be made from this stockpile and applied to the accounts of ordinary mortals to cover their moral overdrafts.

In revolt against the abuses which this system encouraged, the Reformers intended simply to return to the original beliefs and practices of the early Church. Naturally enough they found their strongest ally in St. Augustine, who had already fought a similar battle before them, and whose words even seemed to anticipate such a situation as they now confronted. Naturally, too, since they were risking their lives against the mightiest power in Europe, they applied his doctrines with less restraint and more ruthless consistency than he. Where he had been content to speak of a general corruption of human nature, Calvin coined the phrase "total depravity" (though he occasionally appears to deny it, as in *The Institutes*, book 2, chapter 2, paragraphs 13–16; and chapter 3, paragraph 3). Despite important differences between himself and Martin Luther, on this point they are in essential agreement. The "formulary of concord" speaks for both when it says:

Into the place of the image of God which had been lost there has succeeded an intimate, grievous, most profound and abysslike, inscrutable and indescribable corruption of the whole nature and of all the powers of man, most chiefly of the superior and principal faculties of the soul, a corruption which infects the mind, intellect, heart, and will. Wherefore after the Fall man receives from his parents by heredity a congenitally depraved impulse, filthiness of heart, depraved concupiscences and depraved inclinations.[5]

Luther and Calvin allied themselves even more carelessly than Augustine with the view that sin is something intrinsic to human nature. If this view is epitomized by sentiments like that of the Spanish poet Calderón, "The greatest crime of man is that he ever

[5]Ibid., p. 430.

was born," it finds a close parallel in the following utterances of Martin Luther:

> It is the essence of man to sin.
> Original sin is that very thing which is born of a father and a mother.
> Man, as he is born of father and mother, is with his whole nature and essence not merely a sinner but sin itself.[6]

Variations on this theme continue to recur in Protestant thought. In Sören Kierkegaard's *The Concept of Dread*, for example, it is strongly implied that finite existence necessarily entails sin, and that human freedom is the result of man's fall from grace, a suggestion endorsed by Paul Tillich's contention that human freedom is the point where creation and "the fall" coincide.[7] The most concrete statement is Karl Barth's celebrated dictum, "Before God, man is always in the wrong."

Assuming, for the sake of argument, that such a doctrine could achieve its purpose of precluding self-righteousness, it nevertheless prompts a question which orthodox Protestantism can never satisfactorily answer; namely, how can this conception of human nature as essentially depraved be reconciled with the biblical affirmation of the goodness of creation? Paul Tillich is apparently quite willing to face the implications of the Lutheran doctrine of sin and to grant frankly that finite existence is an evil.[8] Other contemporary Reformation theologians, instead of confronting this difficulty, often seek to circumvent it. This is usually done in one of three ways. The first asserts that self-contradiction, though an embarrassment to the philosopher, is actually a credential of theology, a proof of its transhuman origin. The second contends that the "human nature" which God created was indeed good but bears no resemblance to the "human nature" which we now know. This is in effect a merely verbal solution to the problem. The third seeks to frighten the questioner into silence by branding his inquiries as a mark of intellectual pride. Devices like these, though invoked in defense of God's honor, have the effect of exempting the theologian from the ordinary rules of

---

[6]These expressions were collected by J. A. Quenstedt, *Theologia Didactico-Polemica* (Wittenberg, 1691), Vol. 2, pp. 134f., and quoted by N. P. Williams, op. cit., p. 429.

[7]See Sören Kierkegaard, *The Concept of Dread*, trans. by Walter Lowrie (Princeton University Press, 1946), pp. 41, 97; and Paul Tillich, *Systematic Theology*, Vol. 1, pp. 255f.

[8]See ibid., and also Paul Tillich, *The Shaking of the Foundations* (New York: Charles Scribner's Sons, 1948), Chapters 2 and 8.

discourse. The "theological license" which he thus pre-empts imparts to some Protestant orthodoxy a censorious and even pontifical tone which contrasts unfavorably with the more reasonable tenor of the Roman Catholic.

Originally a pagan doctrine, the conception of sin as intrinsic to human nature imparted an air of pessimism, otherworldliness, and futility to the pre-Christian Gentile world. When combined with the sense of guilt and responsibility as it was in India, it produced the belief that all the world's evils were no more than a just punishment of wicked souls. And this in turn meant that any attempt to alleviate suffering constituted a rebellion against the eternal justice of the universe. The resulting constitutional reluctance to take arms against existing evil, so characteristic of the Hindu, is not without a parallel in Luther. Although he emphatically endorsed a rather rigorous ethic in private life, he taught that great social and institutional abuses, especially by the civil government, were to be patiently endured as the instruments of divine punishment. The powerful grip which this teaching had upon the German mind, and the great difficulty with which some Lutherans finally abandoned it, were dramatically illustrated during the Hitler era.

FREEDOM DENIED

Having tried to put an end to self-righteousness by convicting all men of original sin, Augustine aims another blow at Pelagius's moral hero. He divests him of the power to better his condition by his own effort. His aim, of course, is to deny that man can establish a claim against God. His method is to insist that the situation of man after "the fall" is that of being unable not to sin (*non posse non peccare*). Fallen man, he says, is subject to the "hard necessity" of sinning. His bondage to sin is so great that of himself he can do nothing good.[9]

This denial of human freedom is a perfect illustration of a theory which is propounded in order to combat an error, rather than on its own merits. A spokesman for Pelagius had said that, by the possession of free will, man is emancipated from God.[10] In his radical opposition to such a view Augustine declared that any good deed is due entirely to the "prevenient" grace of God, rather than to one's own will. This

[9] N. P. Williams, op. cit., pp. 364–70, presents a conclusive analysis of the extent to which Augustine did not hesitate to deny the existence of human freedom in any significant sense.

[10] Ibid., p. 356.

grace, moreover, must be "irresistible." Otherwise man would possess a veto over the will of God. As Augustine proceeds step by step to follow the implications of his premises, man becomes more and more the hapless plaything of a capricious deity with a perverted sense of humor. The final upshot is the famous doctrine of predestination, the view that in the counsels of God some men are foreordained to salvation, and others to damnation, and that there is nothing they can do to alter the divine decree. This seemed to Augustine the only way to insure against man's usurping the divine prerogatives. And, just to make sure that nothing human *causes* God to choose as he does, Augustine admits and even insists on the arbitrary, inscrutable, and even irrational character of divine election: "Forbear to set God the Judge in comparison with human things, that God whom we must not doubt to be just even when He does what seems to men unjust, or what, if it were done by a man, would actually be unjust."[11]

Once this position has been stated, its adherents have no choice but to face up to some of its awkward implications. Chief among these, for example, is the radical denial of human freedom. Since, as the Pelagians were quick to point out, the conception of responsibility is meaningless apart from freedom, Augustine hesitated to follow where his own logic led. The result, however, is only some verbal jugglery which, while purporting to solve the problem, in fact only evades it. As N. P. Williams has pointed out, "If we disregard verbal subtleties and concentrate our attention on realities, we shall find that the Augustinian system implies the negation of free-will in any except a highly recondite and unnatural sense of the term."[12]

The Reformers also joined St. Augustine in the denial of human freedom, without which the conceptions of responsibility and guilt are meaningless. With less reserve than he, they championed the doctrines of predestination and the bondage of the will. Thus Luther in his *Treatise on the Bondage of the Will:*

Accordingly this doctrine is most chiefly needed and salutary for the Christian to know that God foresees nothing contingently, but that He both foresees, determines, and actually does all things, by His unchangeable, eternal, and infallible will. By this thunderbolt the whole idea of free-will is smitten down and ground to powder. . . . All things which we do, even though they may seem to us to be done mutably and contingently . . . in reality are done under the stress of immutable necessity if regard be had to the will of God.[13]

[11]Ibid., p. 381.
[12]Ibid., p. 370.
[13]Cited by N. P. Williams, op. cit., pp. 433f.

The utter irrationality of such a deity is not only acknowledged but insisted upon:

In the things of God we must not hearken to reason.[14]

This is the acme of faith, to believe that God who saves so few and condemns so many is merciful; that he is just who at his own pleasure has made us necessarily doomed to damnation, so that, as Erasmus says, he seems to delight in the tortures of the wretched, and to be more deserving of hatred than of love. If by any effort of reason I could conceive how God, who shows so much anger and iniquity, could be merciful and just, there would be no need for faith. . . .[15]

CHRISTIANITY REDUCED TO A DISCLOSURE

There is still another unfortunate corollary of this pre-Christian conception of sin. It forces its adherents to minimize or deny any fulfillment in this life. If sin could be overcome here and now, if *agape* could become a reality of present experience, this would mean that human nature is not incapable of goodness; it would contradict the definition of sin as intrinsic to it. The more tenaciously a theologian clings to this definition, the more radically he will repudiate any palpable effects of Christianity upon human character. He thereby unwittingly puts himself in the position not only of letting theory dictate to fact but of setting arbitrary limits upon the power of God to overcome evil. Symbolic of this tendency is the Reformers' treatment of love. Whereas the Bible, the early Church fathers, and the Roman Catholic Church (including Augustine) unanimously place love at the pinnacle of Christian life, both Luther and Calvin subordinate it to faith. The significance of this inversion lies in the fact that faith can be interpreted (albeit unbiblically) as a special kind of knowledge. As Luther says, "Faith, therefore, is a certain obscure knowledge, or rather darkness which seeth nothing, and yet Christ apprehended by faith sitteth in this darkness."[16] Or, as John Burnaby observes in the case of St. Augustine:

It cannot be denied that faith, in Augustine's general usage of the term, has predominantly the intellectual connotation of the definition which he gave at the end of his life—"to believe means simply to affirm in

[14]Cited by H. Grisar, *Luther*, translated by E. M. Lamond, edited by Luigi Cappadetta, Vol. 1 (London: Kegan-Paul, Trench, Trubner, & Co., Ltd., 1914), p. 216.
[15]Cited by Preserved Smith, *Erasmus* (New York: Harper & Brothers, 1923), p. 350.
[16]Martin Luther, *Commentary on St. Paul's Epistle to the Galatians*, a revised and completed translation based on the "Middleton" edition of 1575. Edited by

thought" . . . "the certitude of faith is a kind of beginning of knowledge."[17]

The whole of Christianity is thereby reduced to a divine disclosure, a special kind of knowledge concerning the "last things." This amounts to little better than a frankly gnostic belief in salvation by knowledge. Its strongest contemporary statement comes from Karl Barth, who declares that any fulfillment beyond mere disclosure, any real transformation of human life, is not only impossible but positively undesirable. In fact, it would "spoil everything."[18] All it would really spoil, what, in fact, it *does* spoil, is Karl Barth's definition of sin. The most devastating rebuttals of his doctrine are the books of C. H. Dodd, who shows conclusively that the early Church stakes its claim on the present experience of the new reality, *agape.*

GOOD WORKS IMPUGNED

Another untoward consequence is the devaluation of good works. Augustine must deny any correlation between an outward act and true goodness; otherwise good works would be "meritorious" and therefore constrain God's favor. In the legitimate effort to guard against the notion that God could be "bought," he resorted to the dubious device of declaring that the divine honor would be offended if anyone but Himself could do good. It is one thing to deny that works are the sole measure of goodness and quite another to declare them irrelevant to goodness. Although Augustine was more reluctant than the Reformers to take the latter position, it follows inevitably from his premises. Goodness becomes solely an inward thing, a matter of "faith alone."[19]

From here it is only one more step to "antinomianism," the theory that it makes no difference what one does as long as one has faith. Since the Christian could scarcely endorse such a position, it is not

---

Philip S. Watson (London: James Clarke & Co., Ltd., 1953), p. 134. Reformation theologians from Luther's time until the present have struggled manfully to avoid the reduction of faith to a kind of knowledge. When the actualization of love as a present experience is denied, however, this is the only remaining alternative, despite all protests to the contrary. This tendency of faith to slide over into knowledge in Reformation theology is an appropriate symptom of its connection with that unchristian outlook which exalts knowledge per se as self-justifying.

[17]John Burnaby, *Amor Dei* (London: Hodder & Stoughton, 1947), pp. 74, 78.

[18]Karl Barth, *The Doctrine of the Word of God*, translated by G. T. Thompson (New York: Charles Scribner's Sons, 1936), p. 180.

[19]Ibid., p. 375.

surprising that Augustine recoiled from it. He, like the Reformers, insists on the importance of good works. The point, however, is not whether they personally urged good works upon their fellow Christians, but whether they did so consistently with the whole tendency of their theology or in defiance of it. As will be argued more fully later, Augustine finds room for good works by insistence only and not by argument. Those who will try to defend him against the charge of antinomianism are always obliged to appeal to his indisputable personal concern for good works, rather than to his doctrines and their fateful import. A more biblical theology, while giving him full credit for his inconsistencies, provides an intellectual framework in which good works have a place *de jure* and not simply *de facto*.

Undoubtedly the Reformation's greatest single embarrassment is its attitude toward good works. Not that the Reformers did not advocate them. On the contrary, they insisted on them. But they would not have had to rely on dogmatic insistence if their own logic had not cut the nerve of good works. Where their opponents made the mistake of implying that mere external observances were a sufficient criterion of righteousness, they themselves fell into the opposite error. They transferred all questions of goodness to a wholly inward realm, a "vertical dimension" in which the soul encountered God, and from which the merely "horizontal" dimension, the external world of space, time, material objects, and friends, was excluded. This cleavage is the basis of Luther's famous distinction between the "two realms" and even of the doctrine of justification by "faith *alone*." Since the Bible gives equal importance to both inner and outer realms, it nowhere uses the phrase "faith alone." In his own translation of the New Testament, Luther inserted the word "alone" gratuitously.

The primacy of the inner world entailed an overwhelming emphasis upon sin as a *state*. Individual sinful acts, being only a reflection of this state, are of little importance. N. P. Williams correctly describes this facet of Reformation thinking when he says that for Luther,

in the last analysis, original sin, the sin of universal human nature as such, apart from the actual sins of individuals, is the only real sin that exists. Actual sin is regarded as being merely an *epiphenomenon*—a loathesome efflorescence of which the foul root is the inherent sinfulness of humanity.[20]

[20]N. P. Williams, op. cit., p. 433.

When the importance of individual acts of sin is minimized, so also, *pari passu*, is that of individual good works. Having once severed the connection between the two realms, the Reformers could never join together what they themselves had put asunder. Hence the famous teaching that law and good works are unnecessary for man's righteousness and salvation.[21] Good works, in fact, have no part in ultimate salvation. They pertain strictly to the sinful state. Luther goes so far as to say that insofar as a man has been made perfect he dispenses with good works. He tries to safeguard against the logical implication of this by hastening to add that in this life nobody is perfect and must therefore submit to the yoke of good works.[22] Having banished the so-called religious dimension to an exclusively inward realm, Luther is swept helplessly along until finally deposited at the logical terminus of the argument which he has started, the famous statement that if a man were not a Christian believer, "all his works would amount to nothing at all and would be truly wicked and damnable sins."[23] When John Wesley encountered this and similar Lutheran utterances, he rightly observed, "Here (I apprehend) is the real spring of the grand error of the Moravians. They follow Luther, for better, for worse. Hence their 'No works; no Law; no commandments.' "[24]

Luther's contemporary defenders can readily point to numerous passages in which he explicitly enjoins good works upon his fellow Christians, such as his *Treatise on the Ten Commandments*. Sydney Cave, for example, cites Luther's *Preface* to St. Paul's Epistle to the Romans, in which he insists emphatically that works and faith are inseparable.[25] This kind of defense absolves Luther *personally* of "antinomianism," but it does not absolve him of responsibility for the logical implication of his doctrines. Their ultimate import is simply that, since all men are essentially sinful, those who act the part at least have the virtue of being honest with themselves, whereas

[21]See Martin Luther, "Treatise on Christian Liberty," in *The Works of Martin Luther*, English translation (Philadelphia: Muhlenberg Press, Vol. 2, 1915), p. 319.

[22]Ibid., p. 328.

[23]Ibid., p. 331. The Anglican Church, which has managed on the whole to steer clear of the excesses of the Reformers, incorporated a similar sentiment in Article XIII of its Thirty-Nine Articles.

[24]See Wesley's journal for June 15, 1741.

[25]Sydney Cave, *The Christian Way* (New York: Philosophical Library, Inc., 1949), pp. 140f.

those who try to be "good" are hypocrites seeking to hide from themselves and from the world their own true nature. Astonishing as such a doctrine is to Anglo-Saxon ears, it is part and parcel of the pagan theory of "salvation by knowledge," in which the only thing to be saved from is ignorance. It has found expression in Germany, not only in the writings of Nietzsche, but in those of Max Scheler, Thomas Mann, and Martin Heidegger. According to Scheler, "the fact that he [the sinner] sins, when he already has a sinful heart, is not evil, but good."[26] Thomas Mann speaks of "a capacity for sin so incurable that it makes a man despair from his heart of redemption—that is the true theological way to salvation."[27] Martin Heidegger echoes the same attitude when he says that conscience, when truly understood, summons man to become guilty.[28]

It goes without saying that to flirt with such pagan notions was the farthest thing from Luther's intention. The point is that they represent the ultimate outcome of a chain of reasoning which had been set in motion by two of his fundamental doctrines, the cleavage between faith and works and the definition of original sin. Short of repudiating these, there is no consistent escape from antinomianism. Unable to extricate himself by argument, Luther resorts to the bludgeon, pronouncing judgment upon those who would follow where his own logic leads. A more recent illustration of the same dilemma, and of the attempt to escape by recourse to epithet, is the following passage from Sören Kierkegaard:

Guilt, like the eye of the serpent, has the power to fascinate spirit. At this point lies the truth in the . . . notion of attaining perfection through sin. . . . On the other hand, *it is a blasphemy* to think that the principle should be carried out *in concreto*.[29]

When the first Roman Catholic missionaries arrived in Japan, they encountered the sect of Amida Buddhism. According to its teaching, all one need do to be saved is to call upon the name of the Buddha. So the Roman Catholics reported to Rome that the Protestants had reached the island before them with the doctrine of justification by faith alone. If one regards only one part of Reformation doctrine, their reaction was perfectly justified. It is an accurate con-

[26] Quoted by Anders Nygren, op. cit., p. 72.
[27] Cited by Robert W. Flint, "Thomas Mann and the Collapse of Bourgeois Humanism," in *Christianity and Society*, Winter 1950–51, p. 24.
[28] Martin Heidegger, op. cit., pp. 287f.
[29] Sören Kierkegaard, op. cit., pp. 92f. My italics.

clusion from that side of Luther's thought which is symbolized by his ill-considered injunction, "Sin boldly." The moral for Protestant theology is this: Beware the man who defines human nature primarily in terms of sin. Out of desperation to prove his point he may be tempted to illustrate it in his conduct. In which case he can readily persuade himself that he is only treating you like the worthless wretch which his doctrine declares you to be.

CONCLUSION

Luther and Calvin, of course, would join St. Augustine in repudiating any such antinomian inference from their primary assumptions. However, if it does follow logically, particularly from the doctrine of "original sin," something must be wrong with their formulation of the doctrine. Their opponents have sensed this, even if they have not often been able to pinpoint the difficulty. If Pelagius's diagnosis never went deep enough, at least he never forgot, as his critics sometimes do, that nothing is more important in the sight of God than what men *do* with their freedom. The argument against Pelagius has all too frequently resembled the behavior of a physician who, correctly perceiving the difference between the cause of disease and its symptoms, forgets that the whole purpose of eliminating the underlying cause is to relieve the patient of the undesirable symptoms.

The historic tragedy was that, while rejecting Pelagius's doctrines, both Augustine and Luther forgot that the purpose of the cure extended to the whole man. At times they even treat Pelagius's emphasis on good works and free will in cavalier, if not contemptuous, fashion. From the fourth century to the present this attitude has only served to stamp Christianity with a fatalistic and otherworldly atmosphere. This spirit is so thoroughly and obviously contrary to the Bible that it continually provokes the spiritual heirs of Pelagius to reassert his doctrines. The Church has thereby been saddled with a perennial dispute, as unnecessary as it is unproductive, between two false alternatives, "faith or works." Each side has been encouraged to stick to its guns by the manifest inadequacy of the other. In these circumstances the only possible victory was a pyrrhic one.

Historically, Augustinianism never has won a clear-cut victory on the level of reasoned argument. In Augustine's own time its triumph was only achieved by the civil government's active suppression of Pelagians. Nevertheless, since, in the absence of a third alternative,

Western Christendom had to choose between Augustine and Pelagius, the former's triumph was certainly fortunate. Pelagius's superficial analysis would have undercut the very foundations of Christianity. The self-sufficiency of his moral titan would have made biblical Christianity irrelevant. According to Pelagius, any pagan might achieve perfection by resolutely performing the works of the moral law. Had this view triumphed, it would have meant the end of the whole biblical understanding of sin and, consequently, of its answer to the problem: *agape*. Within the thought of the Reformers, and especially of Augustine, there are redeeming strands of genuinely biblical thinking. It is these which, when disentangled from the web of pre-Christian ideas in which they are enmeshed, provide the basis for a fresh beginning in theology today.

APPENDIX TO CHAPTER VIII

THE ROMAN CATHOLIC VERSION OF SIN

The Roman Catholic Church, in seeking to avoid the errors of both Pelagius and St. Augustine, has developed a position midway between the two. The question remains, however, whether this is a genuinely biblical alternative, or whether it is merely a makeshift compromise between the two incompatible pagan views. It depends for its plausibility largely upon extremely subtle distinctions, double meanings of words, and a continual shift in perspective.

It makes a significant departure from St. Augustine's doctrine of the fall. Adam was originally endowed with certain spiritual gifts over and above those of a merely natural creature (*donum superadditum*). When, as a result of the fall, this extra, sanctifying grace was lost, man then became a creature of the merely natural order. Then how "sinful" is he? Considered from the merely "natural" point of view, he simply belongs to the created goodness of the world. But there is also a higher, "supernatural" goodness. Considered as a creature who might have partaken of this "spiritual" realm, but who chose instead a lesser good, man is sinful. "The privation of this grace (that is, Adam's original, supernatural endowment), even without any other act, would be a stain, a moral deformity, a turning away from God. . . . This privation, therefore, is the hereditary stain."[30] Though

[30]The Catholic Encyclopedia, Vol. 11, Article on "Original Sin," pp. 314f.

logically vulnerable, this position does have a humanitarian merit. It provides a basis for the official doctrine that infants who die without baptism are sent to limbo, instead of being consigned to eternal damnation, as Augustine would have it.

The attempt to explain how contemporary man can be responsible for an act committed by Adam makes use of similar ambivalence. "If the man, whose privation of original righteousness is due to Adam, is considered as a private person, says St. Thomas, 'This privation is not his fault, for a fault is essentially voluntary. If, however, we consider him as a member of the family of Adam, as if all men were only one man, then his privation partakes of the nature of sin . . .' (*De malo,* book 4, part 1)."

The contemporary position is that, although the man is not responsible in a "strict" sense, he is responsible in a "broad" sense. Similarly, he is not responsible for original sin "in the strict sense of the word but only in a broad sense. Considered precisely as voluntary, original sin is only the shadow of sin properly so-called. According to St. Thomas, it is not called 'sin' in the same sense, but only in an analogous sense."[31] The reader is left to decide for himself whether or not this is equivocal.

[31]Ibid.

CHAPTER IX

AUGUSTINE AND PELAGIUS: BROTHERS UNDER THE SKIN

> Be no longer children, tossed to and fro and carried about with every wind of doctrine.
>
> —Ephesians 4:14

In their eagerness to build a doctrinal dike against any recurrence of moralism, Augustine and the Reformers sacrificed important elements of the biblical understanding of man and God. They developed the doctrine of "original sin" in order to prevent self-righteousness and to dispel the notion that a man could sit down at the bargain counter with God. But the consistent consequence of this teaching is the denial of human freedom, upon which the whole biblical philosophy rests, and of the transformation of men's hearts by the power of the Holy Spirit, apart from which the Gospel is reduced to a disclosure of information about God's plan for the future.

The present chapter attempts to show how Augustine and his successors unwittingly became the victims of a sobering irony. Their costly measures do not even succeed in the purpose for which they were designed. Instead, by a curious inner logic, they lead by a roundabout route to many of the same errors which they were intended to combat. It is especially important to emphasize this point at the present day, when in certain theological circles any criticism of Augustine or the Reformers is apt to be greeted with cries of "Pelagianism." The following pages will demonstrate that Pelagius and Augustine, despite their diametrically opposed starting points, turn out in many respects to be brothers under the skin.

The exposure of an ultimate similarity between such apparently divergent positions will illustrate a principle which Christianity shares in common with philosophy and indeed with any sort of rational discourse: namely, the conviction that, since human reason is part of the created goodness of the world, it will sound the alarm whenever man's thinking is based upon a falsehood. This built-in safety device is the law of noncontradiction: when what a man says in the morning cannot be reconciled with what he says in the afternoon, he must have been arguing from a false premise. The *locus classicus* for the systematic application of this principle are the earlier Socratic dialogues. To state it epigrammatically: no false theory can be consistently elaborated; this is the last laugh which the truth enjoys at the expense of all misconceptions of it. When this principle is applied to the issue under discussion, it means that if, in refuting one error, St. Augustine and the Reformers have fallen into another, they will be led in a circle to the moralistic doctrines they set out to avoid. The following pages will show that this is precisely what happens.

THE METAMORPHOSIS OF PELAGIANISM

The same principle applies to Pelagius. An indirect proof that he, too, begins from a false premise is the fact that, however surprisingly, his position likewise tends to turn into its opposite. The moralist sets out to subdue his evil impulses. But it requires no philosopher to ask, "Where do the evil impulses come from? How did they get there in the first place?" This single question forces the Pelagian a long way in the direction of Augustine. He can only answer that he "came that way," that these impulses are part of his nature. Although this is not yet a doctrine of "total depravity," nevertheless, if the evil impulses are just as much a part of him as the good, then there remains no residual "pure" self which can claim exemption from them. Thus a very direct, logical path conducts Pelagius from his own starting point to Augustine's conclusion.

It is nicely illustrated by some Jewish theology, which from a Christian perspective often seems to err, if anything, in the direction of legalism. The rabbinical tradition produced the theory that man has two equal and opposite natures, the so-called good and evil "yetzers." Some rabbis are even willing to face the logical corollary of this, which is the Augustinian conclusion that God is finally responsible for evil (*o felix culpa!*).[1] The only conclusion consistent with this premise is a rather pessimistic attitude toward a world in which evil has the same status as good. Although Judaism is far too loyal to the biblical emphasis on the goodness of creation ever to allow such an academic consideration to color its positive outlook on the world, the same is not true of most Christian legalists. The Puritan, symbol of latter-day Pelagianism, is stereotyped in the common

[1] See, for example, C. G. Montefiore and H. Loewe, *A Rabbinic Anthology* (London: Macmillan & Co., 1938), p. 295: "Raba said: though God created the yetzer ha-ra (the evil yetzer), he created the Law, as an antidote against it."

mind as the stern executor of the judgment of God upon a wicked world. As R. H. Tawney has so eloquently described him:

Through the windows of his soul the Puritan, unless a poet or a saint, looks on a landscape touched by no breath of spring. What he sees is a forbidding and frost-bound wilderness, rolling its snow-clad leagues toward the grave—a wilderness to be subdued with aching limbs beneath solitary stars. Through it he must take his way alone. . . . Tempered by self-examination, self-discipline, self-control, he is the practical ascetic whose victories are won not in the cloister, but on the battlefield, in the counting-house, and in the market.[2]

Thus does Pelagianism, which appears at the outset so much more positive, hopeful, and optimistic than Augustine, metamorphose into an agent of gloom.

In yet another way, when all the implications of Pelagius's position are consistently drawn out, he lands in the same boat with Augustine. Despite all his protests to the contrary, he is no more able than his adversary to provide for human freedom. This grievous omission is less obvious in his case because he uses a different means to dissolve freedom. Where Augustine sacrifices freedom to determinism and necessity, Pelagius, straining in the opposite direction, reduces it to mere chance. A leading authority summarizes his position thus:

Free will is defined as consisting in a mere capacity or possibility either of good or of evil, that is, pure indetermination, in a mathematical point of uncontrolled and unmotivated spontaneity. We may compare this perfect equilibrium of the will, as the Pelagians conceived it, inclining itself neither to virtue nor to vice, with a balance of exquisite poise, of which the beam remained absolutely horizontal, yet hung with such tremulous delicacy that the faintest breath may incline it either this way or that.[3]

Although at first glance this conception of chance, or indeterminism, appears to be the contrary of necessity, they are but two sides of the same coin. This point has been perceived more clearly by a historian, Arnold Toynbee, than by many philosophers:

Chance and Necessity are the alternative shapes of the Power which appears to rule the world in the eyes of those afflicted with a sense of drift; and, though at first sight the two notions may appear to contradict one another, they prove, when probed, to be merely different facets of one identical illusion . . . the two notions of Necessity and Chance are simply different ways of looking at the same thing.[4]

[2]R. H. Tawney, *Religion and the Rise of Capitalism* (New York: Penguin Books, Inc., 1947), pp. 190–92.
[3]N. P. Williams, op. cit., p. 341.
[4]Arnold J. Toynbee, A *Study of History*, abridgement of Volumes I–VI, by B. C. Somervell (Oxford University Press, 1947), pp. 444–46.

Here is a perfect case of *"les extrèmes se touchent."* The effect upon
the individual is exactly the same, whether his freedom be exchanged
for necessity or for chance. Thus does Pelagius set in motion a train
of logic which does not stop until it has carried him into the
Augustinian camp.

THE NEIGHBOR BYPASSED

Even more startling is the fatal dialectic which likewise drives
Augustine willy-nilly in a direction opposite to the one in which he
intends to go. It is important to emphasize that the following illustrations from the writings of Augustine, Luther, and Calvin are
highly selective. It is equally important to emphasize that this in no
way invalidates them, provided that the *principle of selection* is
legitimate. The principle is simple. It merely asks, what follows consistently from Augustine's starting premises; that is, from his definition of original sin and his attitude toward good works? An inexorable inner logic runs from these points of departure to conclusions
similar to Pelagius's. To be sure, neither Augustine nor the Reformers was willing to follow this logic consistently. One is only too
glad to give them credit for their contradictions. If, however, they
could not say what they wanted to say consistently with their own
premises, then something is wrong with the premises. This, and this
alone, is the point at issue.

A principal cause of Augustine's embarrassment is his failure consistently to define sin as the opposite of love (*agape*). He never rids
himself of the predilection, derived from his saturation with neo-
platonism, to think of perfection in terms of self-sufficiency. The
clue to a man's conception of the highest good is the way in which
he speaks about God. For Augustine, "The Divine life—*amans et
quod amatur et amor*—centers upon itself in ceaseless self-love and
in blessed enjoyment of its own perfection."[5] For man to try to
achieve a similar state for himself is, of course, sin. However, the
reason why it is sinful is not that self-sufficiency is less than the highest good, but rather that it is inaccessible to finite man. The secret
of human beatitude consists in throwing oneself upon God—an act
of faith which paradoxically rewards the "believer" with a sort of
second-degree self-sufficiency derived from God's.

The closest facsimile to God's self-sufficiency which "finite man"

[5] A. Nygren, op. cit., pp. 553f.

can achieve is conceived in terms of knowledge. It is absolute certitude. The demand for certainty as a secure possession underlies the position of both Augustine and Pelagius. Whereas the latter seeks it in terms of an achievable moral standard, the former's conception of it is noetic. Since for him the image of God in man is "the little spark of reason" in him,[6] he not unnaturally conceives human blessedness primarily as a state of perfect knowledge:

Give me what I love. . . . Give me, because I have taken upon me to know . . . This is my hope, this do I pant after, that I may contemplate the delights of the Lord.[7]

His moment of ecstasy with Monica at Ostia he describes as a moment of perfect understanding and speaks of heaven as "that intellectual heaven, where it is the property of the intelligence to know all at once."[8] Luther's writings are permeated by the quest for certitude. One of his touchstones for the truth of a doctrine is whether it helps or hinders the certainty of salvation. Whether or not this ought properly to be called wishful thinking, it does strongly suggest that Christianity merely provides a supernatural way of attaining what the pagan world sought in vain.

Part of the uniqueness of Christianity, however, is its contention that true fulfillment is to be found, not in the splendid isolation of the beatific vision, not in the self-contained certitude of contemplation, but—of all places—in a certain quality of relation between free agents (*agape*). In this relation assured possession gives way to confident trust. For Augustine, however, as for much Reformation theology, the state of "relatedness" is often regarded as a stigma of finitude, something which will be overcome as far as possible by "salvation." The theologian is consequently embarrassed at how to work "the neighbor" into this scheme. He certainly finds no place in Augustine's famous cry, "I long to know God and the soul."[9] St. John of the Cross only pushes this logic one more step when he declares that in the last analysis love for one's neighbor only detracts from one's love for God. By plainly correlating "dealings with men" with the burdensome and oppressive, indeed penal, "works," Luther betrays an attitude not far removed from that of St. John of the Cross. Even at its best, this kind of thinking is unable to imagine

[6] Aurelius Augustine, *The City of God*, Book XXII, Chapter 23.
[7] Augustine, *Confessions*, Book XI, Chapter 22.
[8] See ibid., Book IX, Chapter 10; Book XII, Chapter 13.
[9] *First Soliloquy*, Chapter 7.

love of neighbor for his own sake. The closest it comes is Augustine's comment, "He who in a spiritual way loves his neighbour, what does he love in him but God?"[10]

Augustinian thinking thus arrives by a different route at one of the principal errors of Pelagius. The latter's moralist becomes so engrossed in winning merit for himself that he cannot love his neighbor. The more exclusively he concentrates on winning moral laurels, the more his good works are done out of utilitarian motives. As the Puritan moralist, Richard Baxter, quite frankly says:

> It is an irrational act, and therefore not fit for a rational creature to love anyone farther than reason will allow us. . . . It very often taketh up men's minds so as to hinder their love to God.[11]

At best, the neighbor is merely the object upon which to exercise the virtue of "self-sacrifice." Although Augustine took Pelagius severely to task for this, he fell into the same error himself. As Anders Nygren points out (with thorough documentation), "Love to neighbor is (for Augustine) the ladder on which we can mount up to God. Thus we 'use' our neighbor in order to enjoy God."[12] This description fits Pelagius like a glove.

PHARISEE IN SPITE OF HIMSELF

At a still more surprising point Augustine's attempt to escape from Pelagius reverses itself and delivers him into the hand of his adversary. Despite the polemic by both himself and the Reformers against it, their own primary assumptions issue ultimately in a new legalism. A perfect symbol of this is his notorious contention that one could merit forgiveness of sins by giving alms to the poor. Although such a position seems irreconcilable with his criticism of Pelagius, there is a quite logical explanation. In his attack upon moralism, he concentrated upon the *source* of goodness. He was concerned to demonstrate that no man can do good of himself, but only as a result of the prevenient grace of God. Works done in consequence of such grace, however, he still regarded as meritorious, thus leaving untouched the root error of Pelagius, his definition of goodness in terms of prescribed duties.

The same mistake is repeated by Luther and Calvin, notably in

[10]Which is not even a near miss. Cited by A. Nygren, op. cit., pp. 549f.
[11]Cited by R. H. Tawney, op. cit., p. 202.
[12]A. Nygren, op. cit., p. 552.

their doctrine that God imputes righteousness to the sinner. This is simply a variation of the Roman Catholic treasury of merit. It differs from it, inasmuch as the source of the transferred merit is Christ alone, rather than the saints, but this is secondary to the main issue. The primary objection to the treasury of merit, that which marks it as Pelagian, is that it conceives righteousness in terms of credits and debits. On this point, the doctrine of imputed righteousness has not broken with the medieval Church. It simply assigns all the credit to Christ and nothing but debit to man. Its righteousness may indeed "exceed that of the scribes and Pharisees," but only in a quantitative sense. As Julian Hartt has recently pointed out, " 'exceeds' [in this context] does not mean a more intense form of the same morality—it means a different kind of morality altogether."[13] It means that the entire merit system must give way to *agape*.

Calvin, by contrast, is obliged to argue that God cannot love a sinner until he has first declared him righteous. Aside from involving God in make-believe, this mere "paper transaction" ignores the biblical account of a God who loves men while they are still in their sins. Whether the doctrine of imputed righteousness can be found in the Bible depends upon the interpretation of a few passages of St. Paul. Controversy over this point has too long a history to be dismissed in a paragraph, but the present writer would argue that these passages ought properly to be construed in continuity with the rest of the Bible, rather than in contrast to it.

The reason why they are driven against their will in this direction is their severance of good works, and indeed of all outward action, from the realm of faith. In Luther's emphatic words:

Wherefore since we are now in the matter of justification, we reject and condemn all good works: for this place will admit no disputation of good works. In this matter therefore we do generally cut off all laws and all works of the law.[14]

How can one argue, on the basis of such a statement, that good works ought to be done? This is the insurmountable problem of Reformation theology. Casting about desperately for an answer, they arrive, as a last resort, at a fateful and ironic conclusion. If the self deserves to be punished and scourged, what more effective way to do this than

[13]Julian N. Hartt, *Toward a Theology of Evangelism* (New York: Abingdon Press, 1955), p. 28, note. For an example of the legalism which pervades the doctrine of imputed righteousness, see Calvin, op. cit., Vol. 1, pp. 792ff.

[14]Martin Luther, *Commentary on St. Paul's Epistle to the Galatians*, p. 142.

to saddle him with a set of burdensome rules to obey? In this way his will may be broken and he may learn humility. Hence Luther:

> There are no better works than to obey and serve all those who are set over us as superiors. For this reason also disobedience is a greater sin than murder, unchastity, theft and dishonesty. . . .
>
> [By obeying the first three commandments under parental instruction] the child's own will is constantly broken, and it must do, leave undone, and suffer what its nature would most gladly do otherwise. . . .[15]

Let no one remonstrate that the doctrine of "justification by faith alone" removes any criterion which might enable him to decide *which* "works" ought to be done. The retort is that it is "better for you" to do works *without* a reason than with one. Any reason which you might have would constitute an "ulterior motive." Far more "self-denying," therefore, to do them gratuitously.

The result is a legalism far more grievous than that of Pelagius. He at least had a meaningful rationale for his good works and could draw an objective distinction between better and worse. But under strict Reformation doctrine there is no such rationale. The nature of the deed itself is irrelevant. You only do it because obedience is good for you. This glorification of obedience for its own sake, as a sort of spiritual cathartic, constitutes an open invitation to arbitrary, authoritarian rules. It even suggests that, like castor oil, the more unpleasant the rules, the more beneficial to the victim. According to Luther:

> Therefore God must need take this maul in hand (the law I mean) to drive down, to beat in pieces, and to bring to nothing this beast [the beast, in this case, is resistance to the doctrine of original sin], with her vain confidence, wisdom, righteousness, and power, that she may so learn at length by her own misery and mischief, that she is utterly forlorn, lost, and damned.[16]

This whole line of reasoning bears a startling resemblance to the way in which the tyrannical caste system is justified in India. The argument is that, since ultimately actions done in this life are of no significance, nobody has any ground on which to object to submitting to the requirements of caste.

Luther's exaltation of obedience per se confronts him with a dilemma, for had he not also contended that "a Christian man, if ye

---

[15]Martin Luther, "Treatise on Good Works," in *Works of Martin Luther*, Vol. 1, pp. 250–52.

[16]Martin Luther, *Commentary on St. Paul's Epistle to the Galatians*, p. 303.

define him rightly, is free from all laws, and is not subject unto any preacher, either within or without . . . ?"[17] He resolves his difficulty by means of the fateful distinction between the "two realms." The outer, visible realm is the sphere of law and wrath, while the realm of faith is banished to a completely inner dimension of experience. This totally unbiblical dichotomy, the direct consequence of the fatal separation of faith from works, has persuaded vast numbers of continental Protestants to submit to oppressive external authority as a sign of their indifference to it.

The same tendencies appear in Calvin's thought. "It is of no importance," he says, "what is our condition among men, or under the law of what nation we live, as the kingdom of Christ consists not in these things."[18] Calvin senses the fatal consequence of this cleavage between the realm of faith and the world of everyday life. Speaking of the "regulation of external conduct," he says, "Though the nature of this argument seems to have no connection [sic] with the spiritual doctrine of faith which I have undertaken to discuss, the sequel will show that I have sufficient reason for connecting them together, and, indeed, that necessity obliges me to it."[19] Here, in a nutshell, is the dilemma which Augustine bequeathed to the Reformers. There is no sufficient reason, no necessity, between his doctrine of faith and external actions. It was no more their intention than his to impugn good works. But they accept uncritically his cleavage of human nature into an inner realm, where faith reigns, and the outer world where law prevails. Between these two provinces there is no logical connection. Unable, within this framework, to develop a rationale for good works, they simply dispose of the problem by insistence. To ask for a rationale is to betray stubborn pride. One should be answered not with explanations but with discipline, so that he may acquire the "habit of submission."[20] When obedience is advocated as a good in itself, the objective value of the action can be ignored as it was by Luther:

Now, if it is most reasonable that we should prove ourselves in all things obedient to our heavenly Father, we certainly ought not to deny him the use of every method to accustom us to practice this obedience.[21]

[17]Ibid., p. 138.
[18]John Calvin, op. cit., Vol. 2, p. 771.
[19]Ibid., Vol. 2, p. 770.
[20]John Calvin, op. cit., Vol. 1, p. 433.
[21]Ibid., p. 769.

From this follows a justification of authority per se and a submissive attitude toward social abuse, quite similar to Luther's: "We must obey, because it is unlawful to resist; we must patiently suffer because impatience is a rebellious opposition to the justice of God."[22] Fortunately there is another strand in Calvin's thought which was effec-tively used to justify resistance to oppression. The present purpose, however, is not so much to observe these inconsistencies as to note where he is led by the logic of his primary assumptions.

Calvin went one step beyond Luther in reforging the chain of legalism. Possibly out of a sound suspicion that he had not succeeded in connecting faith with deeds, he added a further incentive to good works. This is the famous theory that, although works have nothing to do with salvation, they are the consequence of it and can therefore be taken as signs that the person who does them numbers among the elect. Though he added a warning against counterfeit, in practice this doctrine hastened the return to a legalism far more strict and relentless than that of Roman Catholicism.

The Reformers are completely unlegalistic in their doctrine of grace, insisting that God in his mercy need not require retribution of the sinner. But what does God forgive: the failure to love, or the disobedience of impossible commandments? Though they are happily not consistent, Luther and Calvin sometimes speak of sin in the latter, legalistic terms. To be sure, this is the very error against which they themselves inveighed. The point is that they did not succeed in articulating a theology which avoids it. G. Ernest Wright calls atten-tion to this discrepancy in Reformation thinking and cites as an il-lustration question 14 of the Westminster Shorter Catechism, which describes sin as "any want of conformity unto, or transgression of, the law of God."[23] He points out that, whenever sin is defined in such a forensic way, the biblical understanding has been obscured. In the biblical view sin is not against a formal, legal postulate, but "is primarily a violation of our personal relationship with God."[24]

Actually the tendency to conceive sin as intrinsic to human nature turns out, under analysis, to be only a special instance of legalism. It amounts to no more than the injunction: "Measure up to a norm which by nature you are incapable of fulfilling." This, at its simplest, is the reason why Augustine and Pelagius are brothers under the skin.

[22]Ibid., p. 775.
[23]G. Ernest Wright, *God Who Acts* (Chicago: Henry Regnery Co., 1952), p. 93.
[24]Ibid.

They agree in conceiving righteousness as a work which man *ought* to achieve by his own efforts, differing only as to whether he is in fact able to do it. The violence of their disagreement on this issue has obscured the far more important fact of their common departure from the biblical conception of goodness as the bilateral relation of love. Augustine's hidden kinship with the very legalism which he combated was inherited by the Reformation. It is beautifully illustrated by the words with which Harriet Beecher Stowe paraphrases the New England Calvinist Jonathan Edwards:

There is a ladder to heaven . . . through which the soul rises higher and higher . . . and changes . . . into the image of the Divine . . . He knocked out every round of the ladder but the highest, and then, pointing to its hopeless splendor, said to the world, "Go up thither and be saved!"[25]

Another similarity between Augustinianism and the position it purports to refute is the repressive attitude of both toward the natural appetites. One thinks of the moralist as engaged in a constant warfare against evil bodily impulses, while the Augustinian and Reformation tradition holds to the insight that sin is spiritual rather than biological. However, the emphasis on humbling the self, when combined with the notion that sin is something which permeates the whole of one's being, easily results in a negative view of physical desires. An easy and practical way to punish the self, and thereby punish sin, is to frustrate them. This is particularly evident in the matter of sex. While Augustine's psychological peculiarities may explain some of his morbid notions on this subject, they cannot account for them all. Though he could scarcely have denounced matrimony and remained a Christian, and in fact praises it, he nevertheless declares that sex and sin, though distinguishable, are not separable. What inevitably corrupts sex is the *desire* which accompanies it.[26]

By contrast, Pelagius always insisted that the natural appetites as such were neither good nor evil, but neutral. He saw nothing wrong with ascribing them to Christ himself. This thoroughly biblical attitude was unfortunately submerged in subsequent theology. Calvin, though he praises marriage, suggests that it is a concession to human frailty and advises, "Let everyone refrain from marriage as long as he

[25]Harriet Beecher Stowe, *The Minister's Wooing* (A. L. Burt Co., n.d.), pp. 49f.
[26]See, for example, St. Augustine, *On the Grace of Christ and on Original Sin,* Book 2, Chapters 40–42. Sören Kierkegaard betrays the same bias in *The Concept of Dread,* p. 44.

shall be capable of supporting a life of celibacy."[27] Although Luther's attitude is somewhat more robust, it is never wholly clear that he does not advocate marriage as a duty to be resolutely performed instead of escaped.

For in God's sight it is a precious and noble good work to train and educate children, to rule wife and servants in a godly manner, and earn one's living in the sweat of one's face, and to endure much misfortune and many difficulties in the person of wife, children, servants, and others . . . How good it is for the soul, although it is an evil for the flesh and its lusts.[28]

The joyous affirmation of the goodness of the present life, so essential to a biblical outlook, could scarcely flourish in such an attitude. Here again the Augustinian position boomerangs. Logically one might expect Pelagius to be the gloomier of the two, considering his unrelieved, humorless preoccupation with self-discipline. Actually, however, it is his opponent's name which has been memorialized in the epithet "Gloomy Gus."

The same fate overtook the Reformation. It began with an outburst of grateful rejoicing in the recovery of "the liberty wherewith Christ hath set us free." Although Luther, despite his gloom, did manage to retain a certain earthly zest for the simple pleasures of life, his over-all estimate of this life is not fundamentally different from Calvin's:

The mind is never seriously excited to desire and meditate on the future life, without having imbibed a contempt of the present. There is no medium between these two extremes; either the earth must bcome vile in our estimation, or it must retain our immoderate love. Wherefore, if we have any concern about eternity, we must use our most diligent efforts to extricate ourselves from these fetters.[29]

Neither official Roman Catholicism nor Pelagianism was ever like this.

THE NEW LEGALISM: SELFLESSNESS

The *faux pas* in Augustine's reasoning, like that of many another philosopher, consists in setting up a double standard of goodness, one for God and another for man. To tell a man, "For God the highest good is self-sufficiency, but for you it is love toward your neighbor,"

27Calvin, op. cit., Vol. 1, p. 439.
28Martin Luther, op. cit., Vol. 3, p. 423 ("An Exhortation to the Knights of the Teutonic Order").
29John Calvin, op. cit., Vol. I, p. 778.

only has the effect of daring him to storm the heavens. Applying the old saw, "What is good for the goose is good for the gander," he finds it more adventuresome, creative, and "courageous" to live by God's standards. It then becomes necessary to scold him for his presumption. He cannot be refuted in argument, because he is, after all, only appealing to the "highest good," that of "God" himself. Since reasoning is futile against him, the only alternative is to suppress him by force or the threat of force.

In biblical Christianity, on the contrary, this problem does not arise. God applies to men his own norm of goodness, *agape*. The thought of Augustine and the Reformers, however, accentuates it, in so far as they insist upon a disparity between God's goodness and man's. It is therefore not surprising to find in their thought a corresponding resort to threats and obloquy instead of reasoned argument. Their invective is directed particularly against the "pride" of man. There is, of course, a sense in which pride properly pertains to sin in the biblical sense, the sense which Reinhold Niebuhr has so vividly brought to modern man's attention. This is the pride of the man whose aim is self-sufficiency. The word can be extended, however, to include any thought or action in which there is the slightest regard for oneself. If sin is defined as "pride" in this sense, it is quite easy to prove that all men are essentially evil. No human act is without some self-reference, if only because it is necessarily the act of an individual self. By means of this definition some contemporary theologians are having a field day pointing out to "prideful modern man" the universality and totality of his sin. As Anders Nygren says, following Luther, "Even *the very highest* which man can seek to obtain . . . is polluted by the egocentricity which is inherent in everything human."[30]

This definition also enables Luther to say, "Man, as he is born of father and mother, is with his whole nature and essence, not merely a sinner, but sin itself."[31] This equation of selfhood with sin makes a virtue of masochism. The way to attack sin is then to mortify the self and its desires. In fact, the poor self stands under a double condemnation. It deserves punishment both for being by nature finite, "related," and dependent, and for having any reference to itself in its actions. To cite Calvin:

For I do not call it humility if you suppose that we have anything left . . . we cannot think of ourselves as we ought to think without utterly

[30] A. Nygren, op. cit., p. 714.
[31] N. P. Williams, op. cit., p. 429.

despising everything that may be supposed an excellence in us. This
humility is unfeigned submission of a mind overwhelmed with a weighty
sense of its own misery and poverty; for such is poverty . . .[32]

Here is another parallel with Pelagius. Ordinarily it is the moralist
who is generally thought of as a man at war with himself, continually
striving to subordinate rebellious impulses to a sovereign will. Since
he is his own worst enemy, the victim of his moral triumph is himself. Hence the self-negation, self-punishment, and self-contempt
which modern psychoanalysis has discovered in the psychology of the
legalist. Erich Fromm describes this kind of "virtue" as "watchdog
morality." Significantly, however, his illustration of it is taken, not
from Pelagius, but from Augustine and the Reformers. For if man is
inherently evil, then the way of virtue is to flagellate himself. In providing a rationale for such self-destructive behavior, Augustine goes
Pelagius one better. The distinction between the "city of this world"
and the "city of God," he says, is that the one is characterized by love
of self to the contempt of God, the other by love of God to the contempt of self.

This sort of thing, in the thought of both Augustine and Pelagius,
is the source of that woeful counterfeit of Christian goodness, the
ideal of "selflessness." To erect selflessness into a virtue is to betray the
pagan origins of one's theology. It is not only a new and more tyrannical legalism but is based on the assumption that any action in
which there is so much as a suspicion of self-reference is wicked. This
is obviously an unchristian bias, for it denies the goodness of creation.
Any action by a free agent has some reference to self, simply because
it is motivated by "my" intentions, "my" purposes. To call this "bad"
is really to find fault with selfhood as such. The Buddhist and the
Hindu quite frankly grant this. Their acknowledged goal is consequently the extinction of the self, for "thine own existence is itself a
sin."

This thoroughly unchristian outlook has so widely displaced biblical conceptions in contemporary thought that one theologian recently
wrote: "The unqualified and unmixed selflessness required by Jesus's
own demand and exemplification of love is both expressed and denied
in every ethical act. The pure fulfillment of the love commandment
is a trans-historical possibility and hope." When selflessness is thus
used interchangeably with love, and the conditions of human existence are consequently declared incompatible with it, the biblical

[32]John Calvin, op. cit., Book 3, Chapter 12, paragraph 6; Chapter 7, *passim.*

standpoint has been left far behind. This grievous distortion issues in the so-called "tragic view of life," so much in vogue nowadays, which current Christian theology is in danger of swallowing whole. According to this view, life is so set up that, in the very nature of the case, one's every action, in so far as it is one's *own* action, is to that extent sinful. It is just such an attitude which would lead a man to say, with Martin Luther, "Sin boldly"—since you cannot help sinning, far better to acknowledge the fact than to affect a hypocritical squeamishness.

The favorite proof text for "selflessness" is the passage about turning the other cheek, in the Sermon on the Mount. Before jumping to conclusions, however, one does well to consider what else occurs in the Bible, passages like:

Think not that I am come to send peace on earth. I came not to send peace but a sword. For I am come to set a man at variance against his father, and the daughter against her mother, and the daughter-in-law against her mother-in-law. And a man's foes shall be those of his own household (Matthew 10:34–36).

Other similar passages concern the expulsion of the money-changers from the temple; the tongue-lashing reserved for the Pharisees; and the weeping and gnashing of teeth which awaits those who reject the good news. There is simply no room in the Bible for a "door-mat" morality, which would have a man reduce his selfhood to the vanishing point.

The Bible takes far too serious a view of evil, and of man's responsibility for preventing it, ever to regard indiscriminate self-surrender with anything but suspicion. If personal compliance were in itself a virtue, one would have no leverage against the sacrifices which Hitler required of the Germans. If turning the other cheek meant simply yielding at all times to the demands of another, it might better be called by a shorter name: appeasement. "Selflessness," in short, is less of a virtue than a rationalization for irresponsibility. It offers a convenient way of avoiding the tough, real-life questions of right and wrong. And, of course, it provides an exquisite instrument for bullying others. If a man can be made to feel guilty for every act which is not "selfless," he can easily be fashioned into a perfect "yes man."

The Christian never allows any such preconceived rule of thumb to dictate his actions. Rather, he assesses each situation on its merits and acts accordingly. In the service of God there are no extremes to which a man may not be called upon to go. He may very well have to turn the other cheek and submit to the will of another. If so, he will not do it for submission's sake. On the other hand, he may be obliged to oppose a given evil with all his might, though not for destruction's sake. Whichever one is called upon to do, to take action against popular evil, or to turn the other cheek, each alternative has its own special pitfalls. Action can be taken with vindictiveness or with the secret intention of simply furthering one's own private ambitions; the other cheek can be turned while one mentally heaps coals of fire upon the offender. It is the *motive* that counts, as well as the deed, before the God who searches the hearts of men. There are no prescribed Christian responses for all possible occasions.

Another way in which self-contempt plays into the hands of the devil has been vividly portrayed by C. S. Lewis. His imaginary Screwtape, undersecretary to the devil, gives the following advice on how to prepare a soul for the kingdom of hell: "You must therefore conceal from the patient the true end of Humility. Let him think of it not as self-forgetfulness but as a certain kind of opinion (namely, a low opinion) of his own place and character." The devil rejoices in such opinions if they "keep the man concerned with himself, and, above all, if self-contempt can be made the starting point for contempt of other selves, and thus for gloom, cynicism, and cruelty."[33]

Perhaps the worst aspect of an ethic of selflessness is its complete misunderstanding of what the Bible means by love. If self-assertion in any form is evil, it is plausible to conclude that love for one's neighbor excludes the love of oneself, that a Christian is to love his neighbor *instead* of himself. Although Augustine emphatically refused to draw this inference, the Reformers make it explicit. According to Luther, "To love is the same as to hate oneself."[34] The contemporary theologian Anders Nygren cites this statement as a great improvement on St. Augustine! According to him, true Reformation theology insists upon the progressive diminution of all self-reference until nothing remains of the individual but "merely the tube, the channel, through which god's love flows."[35]

At this point Reformation theology collides head on with the brute facts of clinical psychoanalysis. Karen Horney, for example, has shown that self-contempt, far from excluding pride, actually accen-

[33]C. S. Lewis, *The Screwtape Letters* (New York: The Macmillan Co., 1944), p. 72.
[34]Cited by A. Nygren, op. cit., p. 711.
[35]Ibid., p. 735.

tuates it: "Self-hate is pride's inseparable companion and he [the patient] cannot have one without the other."[36] Pride and self-contempt are but two sides of the same coin, and the name of the coin is hardness of heart. Granted that the conceited man cannot love, Erich Fromm provides convincing evidence that the same is true of the self-rejecting man. If you do not love yourself, he concludes, you cannot love your neighbor either—unless you redefine love beyond recognition, as some Reformation theologians are not unwilling to do.[37] Love requires that a man be *more* of a self, not less; and it gives him the power to do it. It does not require that a man accord his neighbor the power of veto over him. *Agape* has teeth in it. As an English theologian has said, "God is not merely tender, sympathetic, velvety. In God's love there is an ultimate center and core of rock on which every opposition is smashed to atoms." The "gentle Jesus, meek and mild" is a distortion. The real Jesus, as he is so unmistakably portrayed in the Gospels, stands *for* something. Only because he does is his love worth having.

INVERTED SELF-RIGHTEOUSNESS

The final and crowning irony of the Augustinian position is that it issues logically in a self-righteousness not less repugnant than that which it opposes. It is an example of what Reinhold Niebuhr has called by the telling name, "ideology of conscience"; that is, the attempt to insure virtue by means of a dogma. If only, reasons Augustine, we define human nature in sufficiently unflattering terms, then no one will ever again presume to vaunt himself. Actually pride is no respecter of theories. It applies to the *person* who states a proposition, not to the content of what he says. The truest theory in the world could be held with a secret pride. If it purports to be a sure defense against sin, the result is as predictable as it is ironic. Let a man become convinced that a particular dogma insures him against self-righteousness, and he will brandish it with all the fanatical fervor of the Pelagian flaunting his moral virtue. To fight pride with a theory actually plays into the hands of the devil. It is startlingly instructive

[36]Karen Horney, *Neurosis and Human Growth* (New York: W. W. Norton & Co., 1950), p. 341.
[37]See Erich Fromm, op. cit., Chapter 4, section 1. Ironically, Fromm, too, is finally obliged to redefine love in such a way that it can be achieved by a unilateral effort of will. What finally emerges is simply a thirst for unitive knowledge (*eros*).

to note how regularly the proponents of Augustianism, both ancient and modern, avoid refuting Pelagius on rational grounds and resort instead to epithets like "arrogant," "presumptuous," or "blasphemous." The plain inference, of course, is that "*our* position is the only un-arrogant, un-presumptuous, and un-blasphemous one." Or, to put it still more baldly, "to disagree with us is in itself a sin." Thus does the campaign against pride end by compounding it with intellectual tyranny.

The man in the street, being innocent of such debates, has no difficulty in perceiving the insufferable self-righteousness of the man who indiscriminately declares the sinfulness of all men. This is really a special form of the pride of knowledge. The theologian is "holier than thou" because he knows something about you which you deny. And the cards are so stacked that every denial only "proves" his point. As Reinhold Niebuhr observes, "The recognition in the sight of God that he [man] is a sinner can be used as a vehicle of that very sin . . . the instrument of an arrogant will-to-power against theological opponents."[38]

Not that the theologian exempts himself from the blanket indictment. On the contrary, self-incrimination may become an inverted "good work," his badge of membership in an elite who pride themselves on their acknowledgment of guilt. Erich Fromm discovers exactly this tendency on the part of both Augustine and the Reformers:

Augustine, Luther, and Calvin have described this good conscience in unmistakable terms. To be aware of one's powerlessness, to despise oneself, to be burdened by the feeling of one's own sinfulness and wickedness are the signs of goodness. The very fact of having a guilty conscience is in itself a sign of one's virtue . . . The paradoxical result is that the . . . guilty conscience becomes the basis for a "good conscience" while the good conscience, if one should have it, ought to create a feeling of guilt.[39]

These clinical insights were reduced to the level of everyday experience by a cartoon in the *New Yorker* magazine. Two convicts in the corner of a prison yard are whispering about a third, who is sauntering past with a definitely superior air. Says the first convict to the second, "What I can't stand about him is his guiltier-than-thou attitude." Thus does the Augustinian doctrine of sin amount in the end to self-righteousness in disguise. Because of its ostensible opposition

[38]Reinhold Niebuhr, *The Nature and Destiny of Man*, Vol. I (New York: Charles Scribner's Sons, 1943), p. 202.

[39]Erich Fromm, op. cit., p. 150.

to Pelagianism it can become an even more virulent form of the same thing.

THE CONTRIBUTION OF THE REFORMATION

The present chapter set out to apply to Augustinianism the principle that no false theory can be consistently elaborated. The Christian here shares common ground with the philosophic faith that any false proposition will ultimately encounter the nemesis of self-contradiction. This fate has overtaken the position of Augustine and the Reformers on original sin and salvation by "faith alone." Something must therefore be wrong with these doctrines. The trouble is not far to seek. It consists in the attempt to validate a statement, not on the basis of its truth or falsity, but on moral grounds. This is merely the converse of a fallacy already observed, the attempt to achieve blamelessness by means of a theory. When assent to a proposition becomes a mark of virtue, the net result is the destruction of both truth and virtue. As C. S. Lewis's Screwtape advises his protégé in the art of destroying men, "The great thing is to make him value an opinion for some quality other than the truth, thus introducing an element of dishonesty and make-believe into the heart of what otherwise threatens to become a virtue. . . . Believe this, not because it is true, but for some other reason. That's the game."[40]

Contemporary theologians of the Reformation school look askance at the historical development of orthodox Protestantism. How, they ask, could a movement which began as a protest against legalism and a mechanical conception of virtue have so quickly degenerated into a sterile moralism? Can it be explained as an unfortunate historical accident, or as the failure of later generations to grasp what the Reformers really meant? If the foregoing analysis is correct, such explanations are inadequate. The deterioration of Protestant orthodoxy was due neither to chance nor to human fallibility, but was rather the predictable outcome of the way in which Luther and Calvin formulated two of their principal doctrines: original sin and salvation by "faith alone."

Designed to prevent man from making any claim upon God, these two doctrines severed the realm of external action from the inward, so-called "religious dimension." The effect of this cleavage was to remove any reasonable basis for distinguishing "good" works from "bad." Confronted by the implicit antinomianism of this position,

[40]C. S. Lewis, *op. cit.*, pp. 72, 120.

the Reformers appealed in desperation to obedience per se as a pro-
paedeutic for humility. The result was to fasten upon their followers a
legalism quite as grim as the one from which they had delivered them.
An uncritical return to the Reformation will therefore be less apt to
overcome the ills of Protestant orthodoxy than to exaggerate them.

The truth of this contention is confirmed only too readily by much
of the "neo-Reformation" theology in Europe today, where the historic about-face of Protestantism is being repeated. Side by side with
the attack upon moralism in the name of original sin and "faith
alone" is the dismal reassertion of obedience as the mark of the Christian.[41] When *agape* is mentioned at all, it is often completely recast
in singularly loveless terms. Anders Nygren's brilliant but unbalanced
work on this subject has distorted the thinking of nearly an entire
theological generation.

Nevertheless, the foregoing criticisms would be impossible without
the current recovery of the *spirit* of the Reformation, and without the
positive contributions of Luther and Calvin to Christian life and
thought. These contributions were made under the guidance of their
twofold motto, "scripture and reason." Despite their disparagement
of reason in some contexts, they both extolled it as an instrument of
liberation from oppressive dogmas. They applied it with particular
success to the rediscovery of the riches of the Bible and the early
Church. It is only in collaboration with his unfettered reason that
Luther could say, "Scripture is more ancient and counts for more than
all councils and all fathers."[42]

By continuing to apply reason to scripture, the heirs of the Reformation can develop a genuinely biblical theology, a positive alternative to the pitfalls into which both Augustine and Pelagius were
betrayed. The seed which the Reformers planted might thus come to
full flower.

NOTE

N. P. Williams has shown with convincing finality that, of the five
biblical verses usually recited in support of the Augustinian doctrine
of sin, three have been regularly mistranslated and the other two interpreted with considerable liberty. See N. P. Williams, op. cit., pp. 378f.

[41]For only one example of many that could be cited see Emil Brunner, *The Divine
Imperative*, translated by Olive Wyon (Philadelphia: The Westminster Press,
1947), p. 49.
[42]Martin Luther, *An Exhortation to the Knights of the Teutonic Order*, in op. cit.,
Vol. 3, p. 414.

Part III
Validation of the
Biblical Understanding of Sin

in which it is shown how the Bible fulfills the legitimate intentions of both Augustine and Pelagius and is further vindicated by the facts of everyday experience.

CHAPTER X

AUGUSTINE'S INTENTIONS FULFILLED

> Woe is me, for I am undone. For I am a man of unclean lips,
> and I dwell in the midst of a people of unclean lips.
> —Isaiah 6:5

Within its customary frame of reference the debate between Augustine and Pelagius can never be resolved. Neither side has broken sufficiently with an unbiblical conception of sin. In the Bible the impasse is overcome by the definition of sin as "whatever is opposed to love." It should be emphasized that without Augustine and the Reformers the biblical conception might have remained permanently obscured. Their polemics against Pelagianism are illumined throughout by this and many other scattered insights which go beyond the limitations of their theological premises. By collating and rearranging these passages one can construct the outline of a definitely biblical theology. Kenneth Kirk has in fact noted this in Augustine's case. After observing the many insoluble problems in which Augustine's reasoning traps him, Kirk observes that the germ of their solution is also to be found in his writings:

The solution does not lie, as is often suggested, in his [Augustine's] 'skilful analysis' of the psychology of the will; it is difficult in this regard not to suspect him of ambiguity. It lies in the doctrine that the essence of grace is *love*, and the essence of man's salvation that he should become *loving*. 'Thou tellest of many ways in which God helps us,' Augustine writes against Julian of Eclanum, 'of scriptures, blessings, healings, chastenings, excitations, inspirations; but that He giveth us *love* and thereby helpeth us, thou sayest not.' . . . It [love] is the one force in the world which does not bargain; which leaves the recipient absolutely free to reject, accept, or repay. So, if God's grace is love, its lovingness consists first of all in giving freedom to men and then in keeping them free, if the phrase may be allowed, without any arrière pensée, . . . desiring indeed a return, but never demanding or compelling it. . . . The same power which confers freedom on its recipients also evokes from them—not by contract, nor by force, but by the invincible suasion of a moral appeal,—an answer of love freely given in return.[1]

This leaven of biblical thinking in Augustine's thought would probably have remained buried beneath scholastic logic-chopping but for the Reformers' motto of "back to the Scriptures." Their de-

[1] Kenneth E. Kirk, op. cit., pp. 343f.

termination to recover the original purity of the Gospels informs their own writings with similar passages of well-nigh apostolic power. It also bequeathed to future generations the possibility of the continual rediscovery of the heart of the Christian message. If this process eventually requires a revision of some of their doctrines in the light of a clearer understanding of the Scriptures, the Reformers should be the last to object.

The following pages will show how the Bible provides a viable alternative to both Augustine and Pelagius. Their respective doctrines were developed chiefly for the purpose of guarding against specific errors. They were formulated not so much for what they affirm as for what they deny. With the purposes of both men the Bible largely agrees. It differs in the method of accomplishing them. Its own method fulfills the intentions of each while avoiding their difficulties. Even more than Pelagius, it stresses man's freedom and responsibility, without ministering to self-righteousness or encouraging a moral "rugged individualism." Like Augustine, it recognizes the futility of individual self-saving and emphasizes the initiative of God, without disparaging either good works or human nature as such.

With one of Augustine's aims the Bible does not agree. His purpose in formulating the doctrine of predestination was, at least in part, to emphasize the sovereignty of God over all events. It seemed to him, as to Calvin, an affront to God's majesty to grant that any human action could have an effect upon him. At this point he is still under the influence of the Greek conception of "God" as "impassible." No act of man could "condition" God in any way. The God of the Bible, however, has actually chosen to grant men such power. The culmination of its emphasis upon this is, of course, the crucifixion. This point illustrates beautifully the futility of trying to arrive at knowledge of the biblical God, any more than one would arrive at knowledge of another person, by means of *a priori* deduction. Knowledge of him, like that of other free agents, comes only *a posteriori*, in consequence of what he has said and done.

To Augustine's other intentions the Bible readily assents. It shares his aim of establishing the universality of sin; its existence as an objective fact in the fabric of human affairs; its tendency to perpetuate and aggravate itself; a meaningful context in which to speak of the "bondage of the will"; and the inability of men to extricate themselves by their bootstraps from the situation of hardheartedness. If

the biblical philosophy can achieve these purposes more ef
and by less questionable means, the true Augustinian could o
"Amen."

UNIVERSALITY OF SIN

One of Augustine's primary aims in formulating the doc
original sin was to make certain that no man would consider
exempt from sin. His zeal was undoubtedly stimulated by Pe
contention that it was possible for "good" pagans to have at
perfection even before the time of Christ. Lest any man dec
himself to be in fact immune to sin, Augustine (together wi
Luther) pronounced human nature sinful *in principle*. It thus becomes unnecessary even to be acquainted with the facts of a man's life. He has been labeled a sinner "by definition."

Even if such a solution did prevent Pelagianism, it would do so at too great a price. The biblical alternative, on the other hand, effectively establishes the universality of sin without in any way impugning the human nature which God created. It does this at a single stroke by putting to every man the simple question, "Do you love God with all your heart and soul and mind, and your neighbor as yourself?" This question suffices to convict the whole world. At this point the Augustinian might interject, "But suppose someone answers yes. Then your whole argument is wrecked." If anyone does make such a claim, then God knows whether he is telling the truth.

The Augustinian, in the effort to prove the man a liar, resorts to the definition of sin as intrinsic to human nature. But this is to prejudge the case, and if his antagonist has integrity, such an argument will only intensify his resistance. For instead of appealing for validation to an unbiased examination of the facts, the doctrine invents a "fact" (human depravity) in order to win the debate. The consequence is that to reopen the question becomes itself a manifestation of "sinful human pride." Anyone who does so is sinful by definition. And this, in effect, is only a subtle form of thought control. Ironically, even though the man who professes to love his neighbor as himself may not be telling the truth, it is he who is doctrinally more correct than his Augustinian adversary. For he continues at least to define sin correctly as the opposite of love, instead of as a constitutional blemish on human nature.

By contrast, the Bible defines human nature as in principle "good"

e *capable of love*. The terrible, universal *fact*, however, is that
do not love. This position actually takes sin far more seriously.
s much more grievous if it need not have been than if it is an in-
rent defect. Men might have created a psychic milieu and a social
tructure in which love was fostered. But the grim fact is that they
have contrived to stifle it. The result is a human situation in which
it is at least partially true of everyone that "his hand will be against
every man, and every man's hand against him" (Genesis 16:12).

OBJECTIVITY OF SIN

The Bible not only puts sin on quite as universal a basis as Augustine but also conceives it as objectively operative both in personal
relations and in the structure of society. Where Augustine does so at
the cost of impugning the very conditions of human life, however, the
biblical alternative rests upon a careful analysis of the corporate character of human existence. Spiritually, morally, and emotionally speaking, there is no such thing as an isolated individual. As the Bible puts
it, "We are members one of another" (Romans 12:5; Ephesians
4:25), not in any merely metaphorical sense, but at the most real and
most decisive level. This biblical insight is echoed by contemporary
existential philosophy. As Sartre puts it:

In order to get any truth about myself, I must have contact with another
person. The other is indispensable to my own existence, as well as to my
knowledge about myself. . . . Hence, let us at once announce the discovery of a world which we shall call inter-subjectivity. . . .[2]

Sartre's teacher, Martin Heidegger, also speaks of human life as essentially being-related-to-others (*mit-anderen-sein*), but, although the
fact of human togetherness is acknowledged, a strong negative evaluation is put upon it by both Sartre and Heidegger. It is in fact regarded as a curse.

Such an evaluation is strictly in line with that of the classical
philosopher who regards a splendid isolation as essential to beatitude,
whether divine or human. Where he grudgingly grants the necessity
of a certain amount of social contact, this is strictly a concession to
the limitations of finite existence. The existentialist differs only in
denying that any such self-sufficiency is possible for man.

The Bible, by contrast, regards self-sufficient isolation as destruc-

[2]J. P. Sartre, *Existentialism*, translated by Bernard Frechtman (New York: The
Philosophical Library, 1947), p. 44.

tive and the desire for it as one of the means by which sin perpetuates itself. The pursuit of salvation in terms of independence or "unrelatedness" is something to be delivered *from*. Salvation consists precisely in a special quality of relation between men and between man and God. The structure of human freedom, which entails a relation beyond the self, is thus neither destroyed nor "transcended," but fulfilled. Even God himself, as triune, finds his own beatitude, not in self-sufficiency, but in love.

The Bible's appreciation of the corporate nature of human existence underlies its understanding of sin as an objective reality with which every man must cope. A man is as the sum total of the emotional and volitional relations in which he stands. The spiritual destiny of each is linked to that of his neighbor. Human relations comprise a network carrying positive and negative charges. The impulses which a man receives will generally govern what he in turn imparts to the system. Attitudes of envy, spite, and resentment do not just glance off. They make a lasting emotional dent upon the persons around me. Even if I try to conceal them, and force myself to do "good works" for the other person, modern psychiatry testifies that I can deceive only his conscious mind, not his heart. The tone of voice, the quality of a gesture, the facial expression—all these are telltale signs which the heart does not mistake.

The hostility which they convey has a deadly effect. For he who has been the object of hate will generally pass it along with interest. And he who has not been loved cannot love much. Whether or not I love depends not just on me but partly on my neighbor. And, conversely, my own negative attitude will have a definite effect upon him. Love is a bilateral relation. It takes two to create it, but one is enough to destroy it. To put it bluntly, I possess the rather terrifying power to prevent my neighbor from loving and, consequently, to impede his salvation, as well as my own. I can be instrumental in the hardening of his heart.

Moreover, sin is not just something which men encounter in their personal relations. It becomes imbedded in the structures and institutions of society itself. Slavery is only the most glaring example— and then only because it is not a present temptation. Up until the time of its abolition it did not lack for apologists to justify it on moral grounds. The same is true today of the racial policies of the government of South Africa, just as it was also true of the exploita-

tion of labor during the nineteenth century and before. As R. H.
Tawney so eloquently expresses it:

The doctrine afterwards expressed by Arthur Young, when he wrote,
'Everyone but an idiot knows that the lower classes must be kept poor,
or they will never be industrious,' was the tritest commonplace of
Restoration economists. It was not argued; it was accepted as self-evident.[3]

Among the laws of any nation there will be some which work to
the advantage of one group against another. The sanctity of law is
trumpeted by none more loudly than by those who have made the
laws to serve some special interest. Conversely, where the absence of
a regulative law works to the advantage of a given group, it will be
most vocal in denouncing the right of government to encroach upon
the sacred province of individual liberty. This was true in the days
before the Fair Labor Standards Act and still remains true today in
the case of exorbitant rents charged in tenement houses.

The founders of our democracy were well aware of this tendency
of sin to make use of the social structure for its own ends. The system of checks and balances was designed to prevent any one group
from operating the government to its own exclusive profit. In Lord
Bryce's famous words:

Someone has said that the American government and constitution are
based on the theology of Calvin and the philosophy of Thomas Hobbes.
This is at least true, that there is a hearty Puritanism in the view of human
nature which pervades the instrument of 1787. It is the work of men who
believed in original sin and were resolved to leave open for transgressors
no door which they could possibly shut. . . .[4]

Reinhold Niebuhr, whose writings have done so much to remind
modern America of the realities and reasoning behind democratic
theory, has summed it up in his famous epigram: "Man's capacity
for justice makes democracy possible; but man's inclination to injustice makes democracy necessary."[5]

If any corroboration were needed of the objective reality of sin, on
both personal and social levels of life, it could be abundantly sup-
plied by the clinical psychiatrist. He is constantly thwarted by the

[3]R. H. Tawney, op. cit., p. 224.
[4]James Bryce, *The American Commonwealth*, cited by Reinhold Niebuhr, *The
Irony of American History* (New York: Charles Scribner's Sons, 1952), p. 23,
note.
[5]Reinhold Niebuhr, *The Children of Light and the Children of Darkness* (New
York: Charles Scribner's Sons, 1949), p. xi.

futility of sending his patients back into the "continuum of neurosis" —that is, a milieu in which they will once again be at the mercy of malevolence and discord. Since love requires two persons to sustain it, but can be destroyed by one, it is at a constant disadvantage. The wonder is that it has not long since been squeezed entirely out of the system.

SELF-PERPETUATION OF SIN

The biblical alternative also explains how, when once started, sin tends to aggravate and perpetuate itself. Assuming, for the sake of argument, that sin (in the biblical sense) is a fact, then the most important question would be, "Is forgiveness possible?" If it were, then the necessary preliminary to it would be *repentance*. Repentance, however, is the one thing that men involved in sin find most difficult to accomplish. They will go to any lengths to avoid it. The most obvious alternative to repentance is simple self-justification, the refusal to admit one's complicity in sin. If the person who thus pleads innocent is in fact really sinful, then he will be susceptible to a gnawing sense of guilt which belies his claims. He may succeed in repressing this feeling, in driving it out of his consciousness, but it remains within him all the same. In fact, it operates even more effectively in the dark. It will drive him to prove, both to himself and to others, that he really is as virtuous as he pretends. As the history of Pharisee and Puritan proves, there is nothing more fatal to human relations than the man whose primary concern is to establish his own moral goodness. His favorite method is to do so at the expense of others. A direct path leads from this technique to the persecuting fury of the inquisitor or witch-hunter. Having once established a foothold, sin thus proceeds to capture by stealth many whom it could not take by storm. Men appeal in all sincerity to illusory virtues as the justification for their atrocities. This analysis of the "inner dynamics" of sin brings out its close connection with deception, especially self-deception. As Reinhold Niebuhr has expressed it:

The desperate effort to deceive must, therefore, be regarded as, on the whole, an attempt to aid the self in believing a pretention it cannot easily believe because it was itself the author of the deception. If others will only accept what the self cannot quite accept, the self as deceiver is given an ally against the self as deceived. All efforts to impress our fellow men, our vanity, our display of power or of goodness, must, therefore, be regarded as revelations of the fact that sin increases the insecurity of the self by veiling its weakness with veils which may be torn aside. The self is afraid of being discovered in its nakedness behind these veils and of being recognized as the author of the veiling deceptions.[6]

It is thus no accident that the Bible speaks of the devil as the father of lies. It is a lie that first causes Eve to put her trust in a false god, and it is only by means of a compound falsehood that men continue to avoid repentance. The more they do this, the farther they are from repentance, and the more vulnerable they become to intensified assault from evil. Just as the deadliest diseases are those which cause no warning pains, so also does sin destroy its victim by blinding him to its reality. As Denis de Rougement remarks, the devil's greatest triumph is to convince men that he does not exist.[7] Hence Christ's message found a readier reception among publicans and sinners, who knew they needed forgiveness, than among the scribes and Pharisees who did not.

The rather startling implication of this position is that in some very important areas of experience man knows only so much as he wants to know, that his reason is in fact the instrument of his will. If this is true, the goal of perfect knowledge, to which men have aspired from the days of ancient Greek philosophy to the present, can in principle never be reached without a prior reorientation of the will. Sin begets ignorance. Therefore knowledge must wait upon the overcoming of sin, which in turn is dependent upon forgiveness. This close correlation of sin with lack of understanding is made explicit in such biblical passages as the following:

Perceive ye not yet, neither understand? Have ye your heart yet hardened? (Mark 8:17.)

For they considered not the miracle of the loaves: for their heart was hardened (Mark 6:52).

If this is true, then it is at least possible that some of the most imposing systems of knowledge the world has known, whether philosophical or scientific, are in fact "rationalizations" devised with the partial, if unconscious, aim of rendering sin impossible and repentance unnecessary. Not that this intention would necessarily disprove any such system. But its recognition does free the student to

[6]Reinhold Niebuhr, *The Nature and Destiny of Man*, Vol. 1 (New York: Charles Scribner's Sons, 1943), pp. 206f.

[7]Denis de Rougemont, *The Devil's Share*, translated by Haakon Chevalier (Washington, D.C.: The Bollingen Series Two, 1944), p. 17. De Rougemont is quoting the poet Baudelaire.

examine on its merit, instead of accepting on authority, either the oldest or the latest theory concerning the nature of reality and man's place within it.

In addition to the technique of openly denying the fact of sin, there remains a more subtle method of avoiding repentance: that of repenting for the wrong thing. In order to do this, one must first devise an unbiblical definition of good and evil. For the Bible nothing is more real than the direction, quality, and expression of the wills of men. The decisive transaction between God and man, and between man and man, occurs in this sphere. What a man ought truly to repent of is determined by the question, "Do you love God with all your heart and soul and mind, and your neighbor as yourself?" In an effort to deflect the judgment of God from this most crucial area, men can invent all manner of "sins" to repent of. They can regard "works alone" as decisive and deplore their failures on this level. Or they can regard "faith alone" as decisive—a position which often tends to substitute indiscriminate self-abasement for concrete acts of repentance. Or they can (and probably will) dismiss the biblical emphasis on the heart as sheer sentimentalism.

If the biblical conception is the true one, then these alternatives merely enable a man to avoid repentance. The result would be a residue of unacknowledged and unforgiven sin which could poison the entire personality—the kind of "floating guilt" which has such a crippling effect on the psychiatrist's patient.

Its destructive consequences are dramatically illustrated by the latest reports from former prisoners of the Communists during the Korean War. A man in solitary confinement was told repeatedly and authoritatively, "You know you are guilty. Confess." These words found their target. By playing upon his ill-defined and repressed sense of guilt, his captors were able to extort the most outlandish "confessions." Thus does sin become the instrument of its own increase.

Another disastrous consequence of unacknowledged guilt is that it compels men to find a scapegoat. They try to banish the subconscious sense of sin by projecting it onto others. Hitler's charges against the Jews are a notorious example. Another would occur closer to home if ever the search for spies and traitors were to become a national pastime. The popularity of such a morbid game would not be due primarily to a genuine concern for the national security. The secret of its appeal would lie in a subtle exploitation of every man's desire to dispel his misgivings about himself. The standard way to inflate one's own sense of virtue is, of course, to find a culprit at whom to hurl vindictive recrimination. The new sport would supply a morally uncertain generation with a spurious good conscience by insinuating the tacit slogan, "Every man a moral vigilante." It would offer men a pretext to indulge in an orgy of "outraged public opinion." Like the Saturnalia of ancient Rome, this latter-day mass orgy would require a steady flow of victims. The manner of their selection would be merely incidental (though a preference for Christians might still be detected). Men obsessed with proving their own righteousness will stop at nothing.

BONDAGE UNTO SIN

The biblical understanding of sin accomplishes another of Augustine's purposes by providing a meaningful sense in which to speak of the "bondage of the will." If human freedom is only *fulfilled* in *agape*, then, conversely, it will be progressively *destroyed* by sin. How dreadfully true this is can again be confirmed by a glance at the clinical data of the psychoanalyst. His patients repeatedly testify to the effectiveness with which an environment of submerged hostility can impair the exercise of freedom. Though they might *like* to establish harmonious relations with their neighbors, they simply cannot. The psychiatrist knows better than merely to recommend a "genuinely friendly overture" as a sufficient remedy. In the first place, the word "genuinely" presents a stumbling block. Many such ostensible overtures are in reality no more than attempts to put the other party "one down" by a show of superior virtue. D. H. Lawrence understands this perfectly in an episode in his novel, *The Rainbow*. In the midst of a quarrel with her sister Ursula decides to try "the Gospel ethic" and smugly presents her cheek for her sister to slap. Whereupon Theresa lands a resounding wallop directly on target—to the reader's immense satisfaction.

In the second place, suppose a sincerely friendly gesture were made. Whoever initiates it makes himself vulnerable. In an atmosphere already heavy with spite the chances are that such voluntary exposure will constitute an invitation to sadism. The net result will only be to aggravate the situation. Both parties have lost the freedom to break out of the vicious circle of mutual hostility. So deep are the resentments on each side that a "friendly overture" is apt to be either insincere or abused. It is more than a mere metaphor to say that both are in bondage to the powers of darkness.

At this stage one still retains the freedom to elect alternatives, to do external acts of service and kindness, and to avoid overt rudeness and brutality. The creeping paralysis of freedom can proceed still further, however, until in certain circumstances one ceases to act voluntarily at all. These are the instances of "compulsive behavior," in which a person simply cannot help squelching his wife, or perhaps making a public fool of himself, like the buffoon of Dostoevski's novel *The Brothers Karamazov*. He can say with St. Paul, "The good that I would I do not, and the evil that I would not, that I do." (Romans 7:19.)

Compulsions like these have established a bridgehead in the behavior of most of us. When they extend their dominion over a sufficiently large area of the personality, the person is pronounced psychopathic. His freedom has been taken captive by the powers of evil, and he is no longer accountable for his actions. He can no more liberate himself than a man in chains.

LIMITATIONS OF SELF-HELP

The fifth purpose which the Bible shares with St. Augustine is to show that man cannot deliver himself by his own efforts alone, apart from God. The necessity for God's initiative has been so thoroughly implied in the foregoing pages that little need be added. Men have contrived to entangle themselves in a web of enmity extending from camouflaged rivalry to overt conflict. Once this pattern has been established there is no simple way out. The hermit, though his view of salvation is fallacious, at least sees this much. Even where genuine love does continue to brighten the picture, its flickering light is constantly at the mercy of sin.

The situation can be retrieved only by love, but love is not man's to command. Who by taking thought can love his neighbor as himself? This question thrusts home the bolt against Pelagianism. In order to love one must first *be* loved from beyond oneself. The only possible solution would be Someone whose love could survive the worst that men could inflict. The vicious circle might then be broken, if such a One directed his love toward men. If they could allow themselves to respond to it, they might find their own long-dormant capacity to love mysteriously awakened. This would in fact be one of the marks of all who had encountered such an unconditional love from beyond themselves. The result would be a new kind of community, one in which the forces of hostility had been deprived of their advantage. Such a community would constitute a bridgehead from which to wrest from these forces the control which they have so long exercised over men. In the course of the conflict it too would undoubtedly experience the destruction of love, but it would also have the resources for its continual renewal. Such a community is not in man's power to create. It would indeed require a "new creation." "With men, this is impossible. But with God, all things are possible" (Matthew 19:26).

ALTERNATIVE TO SELFLESSNESS

One final question remains to be answered. Is the conception of sin as idolatry able to account for the extremes of megalomania, cases in which a person's whole life appears to be centered, not upon any external idol, but upon sheer self-aggrandizement? Is not the conception of sin as self-centeredness a more adequate interpretation of the diabolic craft and calculated ruthlessness which are writ large in such lives and have doubtless presented a temptation to nearly everyone?

According to the biblical view, what distinguishes even the most involute self-seeker from the "saint" is not simply the pursuit of self-interest, for this is part and parcel of human freedom. Rather, the two are distinguished by the terms in which they *conceive* their self-interest; that is, by the respective gods whom they trust to fulfill it: the false gods of prestige and power, or the God who can soften the hardened heart. Seen in this light, complete self-centeredness is impossible, and apparent self-centeredness is not a cause but a symptom.

This position finds partial confirmation in the fact that the really perverse self-seeker, the one who seems actually to lead a vampire existence by undermining of others, often does not even recognize this picture of himself. He may make no explicit claims for himself at all and be the first to denounce selfishness in others. Having been blinded by his false gods, he is horrified at the thought of its being attributed to him. His self-centeredness is not the cause of sin but rather the unintended by-product of idolatry.

His counterpart is the person who consciously and defiantly proclaims a policy of exclusive self-worship. He could learn a lesson from the mystics. They know that the mere fact of human freedom involves the agent in a relation beyond himself and that the only escape from this situation is consequently the annihilation of the individual (see Chapters V, VII). They could have warned him that the pursuit of self-sufficiency in any less radical way would issue in the exact opposite of its intention. And this is precisely what happens.

The egomaniac's drive toward self-sufficiency has the effect of making him the most pathetically dependent of men. By seeking power and glory at the expense of his fellows, he becomes parasitic upon them. He is willing to humiliate himself in order to extract what he wants from them, be it their money or their praise. The Byrons and the Nietzsches, who make such a show of contempt for mankind, are not above the whining complaint that they are not sufficiently appreciated. This dependence of the self-seeker upon his own victims is analyzed by George Eliot:

He did not care a languid curse for any one's admiration; but this state of not-caring, just as much as desire, required its related object—namely, a world of admiring or envying spectators: . . . a rudimentary truth which is surely forgotten by those who complain of mankind as generally contemptible, since any other aspect of the race must disappoint the voracity of their contempt.[8]

Moreover, if one defines sin as the tendency toward "me first," then the opposite of sin, or virtue, becomes "me last." As shown in the preceding chapter, such an ethic of selflessness not only turns into an inverted "me first" again but also becomes a new and deadly legalism. The Christian allows no such rigid formula to prescribe his actions in advance. Rather, he assesses each situation on its merits and acts accordingly. But his action is by no means capricious or without principle on that account. On the contrary, it achieves a greater consistency precisely because it is not based upon a fixed law. Literal and slavish devotion to a law will ultimately lead to deeds which defeat the spirit of the law (this is treated more fully in Chapters XII and XIII). True consistency is achieved by loyalty to the *intention* of the law. And this, in turn, is based, not upon some inflexible principle, but upon constancy of purpose. As the Bible calls it, the steadfast will of God.[9]

Of course, for such an ethic to make sense, one must take God se-

[8]George Eliot, *Daniel Deronda*, Vol. 2 (New York: Doubleday, Page & Co., 1901), p. 196.
[9]Sören Kierkegaard called this by the misleading phrase, the "teleological suspension of the ethical." It ought rather to be called the transposition of the ethical norm from fixed rules to the steadfast will of God.

riously. Some theology, on the contrary, gives the impression of trying to see how much of Christianity could be salvaged, how close a facsimile could be devised, if God were left out of account. The answer, obviously, is that without God nothing at all would remain of Christianity. After all, it would be a paltry God indeed whose exclusion made no appreciable difference to human undertakings, whether practical or philosophical.

CONCLUSION

The biblical alternative thus accomplishes all that Augustine intended by his doctrine of original sin, without falling into a disparagement of human nature as such. A man is as the quality of the volitional attitudes which impinge upon him. A newborn infant who came into the world completely without sin would still be inevitably affected by the emotional environment in which we all live—a milieu which any psychiatrist can testify is thoroughly shot through by strategies and structures of malice. From the moment of birth he becomes a victim, not of a defective human nature, but of what man has done to man. Obliged to fend for himself in such a world, he then grows up to become a party to the perpetuation of hardheartedness in his own right.

Augustine's intention can thus be achieved without postulating an inherited taint or an essential corruption of human nature. These doctrines do represent sincere efforts to reflect upon the implications of the biblical message and actually to prevent distortions of it. But, if these same purposes can be accomplished in a way which is both more reasonable and more biblical, there is no need to cling to them. In fact, the reluctance to let them go would betray either an essentially pagan conception of man or else the perennial tendency to make an idol of a doctrine, to distort the facts to fit a preconceived theory.

CHAPTER XI

PELAGIUS'S INTENTIONS FULFILLED

> Whosoever doeth not righteousness is not of God, neither he
> that loveth not his brother.
>
> —1 John 3:10

Having accomplished the five primary aims which it shares
with St. Augustine, the biblical alternative must now confront
Pelagius. It must explain how it can at the same time fulfill the two
great purposes for which he fought: the preservation of responsibility
in a meaningful sense (and not just in name only); and a case for
good works based upon a consistent rationale, rather than upon
gratuitous insistence. Considering how much has already been con-
ceded to Augustine, Pelagius might well be skeptical of the outcome.

JOINT RESPONSIBILITY

The question of responsibility will be considered first. If the
reason why one does not love is that one finds himself in an unloving
milieu, how can he be held accountable? The answer does indeed involve a break with the view, as modern as it is Pelagian, that responsibility is an entirely individual matter. For the Bible it is always
mutual. Although foreign to contemporary thinking, this conception
is entirely consistent with the biblical outlook as a whole. For the
Bible nothing is more real than what happens *between* selves. The
conception of moral self-sufficiency, of an individual monad working
out a solitary salvation in isolation from his emotional environment,
is as alien to the Bible as it is to the psychiatrist. Man is what he is
largely in terms of his emotional and volitional relationships.[1] Though
not widely held at present, there is one alleged fact which, if true,
provides this conception with dramatic proof, thereby making individualistic theories appear superficial in comparison: namely, the
"wolf-children" occasionally reported from India. According to reports, these pathetic creatures offer positive proof that, without human
companionship, man quickly becomes a beast indeed. Their rehabili-

---

[1] No one is more responsible for the recovery of this understanding than Martin
Buber. G. Ernest Wright's most recent book, *The Biblical Conception of Man in
Society* (London: SCM Press, 1954), also makes a significant contribution to the
subject.

tation, even after years of human society, has never been complete.

If man only becomes man in community, then it is not unreasonable to speak, as the Bible always does, of his communal destiny. This conception emphatically does not transfer all responsibility from the individual to an abstract, impersonal entity like "the state." This would only make the state a scapegoat for sin which belonged properly to you and me. The point is rather that they are *shared* sins. Each individual bears responsibility but not an exclusive responsibility. A classic example of this outlook are the words of Isaiah: "Woe is me, for I am undone. For I am a man of unclean lips, *and I dwell in the midst of a people of unclean lips*." (Isaiah 6:5.) The prophet's own responsibility is inseparable from that of his compatriots.

The moral confusion of our own time is partly due to the loss of this biblical understanding. This was never more strikingly illustrated than during the British Parliamentary debates in 1948 on the proposal to abolish the death penalty. Those who opposed the death sentence based their case on the argument that, since the individual was merely the product of his environment, he could not be held responsible for his crimes. The death penalty was therefore held to be unfair. The other side rightly discerned the disastrous implications of this sociological determinism. They were obliged to link their defense of responsibility, however, with the retention of the death penalty.

Actually, both sides were arguing from the same fallacious premise: namely, that, if there is any such thing as responsibility at all, it must be understood in a strictly individualistic sense. Opponents of the death penalty detected the injustice of holding the criminal solely responsible and were therefore willing to abandon the only kind of responsibility they could conceive of. Their antagonists likewise could imagine no other kind of accountability and were therefore forced into the position of linking responsibility to the death penalty. Here is the point at which the biblical view becomes supremely relevant. On the one hand, as against the determinists, it would insist on the responsibility of the criminal. But, on the other hand, it would also insist that this responsibility be shared by the community as a whole. To commute the sentence to life imprisonment therefore puts the responsibility squarely where it belongs: upon the criminal himself, to be sure, but also upon every member of the community. All are responsible for tolerating conditions which are conducive to crime. Therefore, all ought to contribute to the support of the offender during his imprisonment, as well as to the attempt to rehabilitate him. His execution would merely enable them to ignore their own complicity in the sin, to transfer to a scapegoat the guilt in which all share.

Brethren, if a man be overtaken in a fault, ye which are spiritual, restore such an one in the spirit of meekness; considering thyself, lest thou also be tempted. Bear ye one another's burdens, and so fulfill the law of Christ (Galatians 6:1-3).

It might still be objected that, if the conception of joint responsibility is true, it is impossible to determine the size of each person's share. This difficulty, however, is more of an advantage than otherwise. It provides a theoretical framework within which no man can either boast of his own sinlessness nor confidently calculate his brother's share. Nor can he attempt to attain purity by seceding from the human race. As to the final apportionment of responsibility, the Bible has a ready answer, albeit one which, like the rest of Christianity, only "works" when God is taken into account. One of its favorite themes is that, although the human heart may be hidden from man, it is an open book to God:

For the word of God is quick, and powerful, and sharper than any two edged sword, piercing even to the dividing asunder of soul and spirit, of the joints and marrow, and is a discerner of the thought and intents of the heart. Neither is there any creature that is not manifest in his sight: but all things are naked and open unto the eyes of him with whom we have to do (Hebrews 4:12-13).

By breaking with the idea that responsibility is entirely an individual matter the Bible by no means destroys the conception of responsibility as such. On the contrary, it intensifies it. Whereas Pelagius encourages a man to cut the ties that link him to his fellows, the Bible never lets him forget that his responsibilities extend far beyond an imaginary island of private morals. Only so will he truly understand what it means to pray, "Forgive us *our* trespasses."

GOOD WORKS DE JURE

It remains to show how the Bible accomplishes the second purpose which it shares with Pelagius, the provision of an adequate rationale for good works, without making his mistakes. His own incentive to good works rests upon the belief that by means of them a man can bargain his way into heaven. Augustine and Luther rightly reject this motive. But it is as though they cannot conceive of good works being done for any other reason. In that event the only alternative would indeed be to disparage good works as such. The result would be an excessive self-scrutiny which either shrinks from helping the neighbor for fear of an impure motive or else refuses to discriminate between good and bad works on the ground that they are all impure anyway. This morbid scrupulosity is, in fact, another point at which neither Augustine nor Luther has broken sufficiently with Pelagius. Their writings, like the moralist's, reflect an excessive preoccupation with self.

The biblical alternative is to restore *love* to its primacy. Once this is done, then good works, though they cannot save a man, remain well-pleasing both to God and neighbor. This is a sufficient motive for doing them. St. Paul says, "Although I give my body to be burned, and have not *agape*, it profiteth me nothing." (1 Corinthians 13:3.) Though indeed it profit *me* nothing, it may nevertheless be what God wants done. Nor need the Christian be deterred by a possible mixed motive. Rather, he asks God's forgiveness for it. Even when he cannot love, a good deed can stand as a concrete token of the "good that I would." A Christian does good works, then, not in a spirit of "what a good boy am I," but rather, "Lord, have mercy—I had to do it more from duty than from *agape*."

This is one half of the biblical rationale for good works. The other is that, although they cannot by themselves create love, "bad works" can destroy it. Since love is a bilateral relation, not simply a one-way efflux, it follows that whether or not my neighbor loves me will depend partly on me. On the level of personal relations the most obvious obstacles which I can erect are acts of insolence, contempt, patronage, deceit, and the like. Conversely, acts of respect and courtesy, while unable in themselves to generate love, do at least provide a milieu in which it is possible.

On the level of society as a whole it has been established statistically that certain economic conditions and policies are the breeding ground of resentment and hatred. While it has also been shown that improvement of these conditions does not in itself effect a miracle in the heart of man, it can at least remove some of the impediments to a harmonious society. Although "nothing can separate us from the love of God," we can still separate ourselves and each other from him. One of the most effective ways of doing this is to acquiesce in institutions or laws which tend to perpetuate, rather than ameliorate, human misery.

This is the basis of Christianity's explosive social dynamic. A Christian is, by definition, one who has an intense concern for problems of justice on all levels of communal life, whether economic, political, or social. Those who urge the Church to "mind its own business" and to confine itself to "saving individual souls" are in fact addressing themselves to a different religion. For Christianity, since we are members one of another, there is no such thing as individual salvation. Rather, the volitional health of the individual is inseparable from that of his neighbor. A sore spot in the body social is consequently of more than passing concern to every one of its members. Whether they know it or not (and, if they do not, the Church ought to remind them), the affliction of a part of society does in fact discharge the venom of resentment and vindictiveness into the emotional fabric of the whole. The classic New Testament expression of this is the figure, "many members yet one body" (1 Corinthians 12:20).

The potent implications of this metaphor were vividly pointed out in a recent address by Sir George McCleod on the subject of religious healing. It is both foolish and blasphemous, he said, to pray for an indigent person's recovery from tuberculosis as long as one remains indifferent to the noxious housing conditions where the disease is bred. This statement stands in the direct line which stretches all the way back to the Hebrew prophets. None is more eloquent than Amos:

They sold the righteous for silver, and the poor for a pair of shoes. . . . For as much therefore as your trading is upon the poor, and ye take from him burdens of wheat: ye have built houses of hewn stone, but ye shall not dwell in them; ye have planted pleasant vineyards, but ye shall not drink wine of them. . . . They afflict the just, they take a bribe, and they turn aside the poor in the gate from their right. . . . But let judgment run down as waters, and righteousness as a mighty stream" (Amos 2:6; 5:11,12,24).

The twentieth-century reader of these remarkable words will scarcely be surprised at the reaction which they produced when they were first uttered. The high priest reported to the king that Amos was subversive (7:10).

A defender of the extreme Augustinian position might here recoil in horror at the thought of works being admitted to the realm of redemption. This only betrays a lapse into a legalistic conception of good works. Such a definition would indeed tempt men to try to achieve goodness by their own efforts and would correspondingly evoke the theologian's strictures. John Wesley detected this tendency in Martin Luther when he remarked of the latter's *Commentary on Galatians,* "How blasphemously does he [Luther] speak of good works and of the law of God."[2]

When, on the contrary, goodness is conceived as a quality of relation between persons, then "works of the law" can be seen in their proper perspective and appropriated to serve the ends of *agape.* Actually the strong biblical emphasis on the unity of human personality makes it impossible to speak of love apart from deeds. Love is only fully actualized in actions. If man is the "psychosomatic" unity which the Bible declares him to be, then, Augustine to the contrary notwithstanding, a further conclusion inevitably follows. Not only do one's inner feelings influence one's outward actions, but the converse may also be true. External acts *may* affect the orientation of the heart. There is no reason in principle why they could not contribute to *agape,* always granted that they can never generate it by themselves alone.

It is no accident that the clearest expression of this biblical truth in our time should come from the Hebraic tradition. Rabbi Abraham Heschel has expressed it with characteristic eloquence:

Faith is but a seed, while the deed is its growth or decay. Faith disembodied, faith that tries to grow in splendid isolation, is but a ghost, for which there is no place in our psychophysical world. . . . Religion cannot be divorced from conduct. Judaism is lived in deed, not only in thought.[3]

One should always do the good, even though it is not done for its own sake. It is the act that teaches us the meaning of the act. . . . Serving sacred goals may change mean motives. . . . There is power in the deed that purifies desires. It is the act, life itself, that educates the will. The good motive may come into being while doing the good.[4]

If this sounds like Pelagianism, it is only because one has still failed to throw off the tendency to think of goodness in forensic terms.

[2]See John Wesley's journal for June 15, 1741.
[3]Abraham Heschel, *Man's Quest for God* (New York: Charles Scribner's Sons, 1954), p. 110.
[4]These lines were taken from the manuscript copy of Dr. Heschel's chapter in the forthcoming volume, *The Theology of Reinhold Niebuhr* (New York: The Macmillan Company). An excellent criticism of the doctrine of justification by "faith alone" is the chapter of that title in Walter Lowrie's *What Is Christianity?* (New York: Pantheon Books, 1953).

When one realizes that the law was made for *agape*, and not man for the law, it loses its tyrannical character and becomes the servant of love. The ramifications of this insight on the social plane having been discussed above, it remains to apply it to person-to-person relations. The best illustration is the subject of good manners, which, in fact, contains the whole problem of "good works" in miniature. Manners are currently in retreat before the leveling effect of a purely scientific world view. Our own intellectuals sometimes seem to echo the Communist taunt that manners are simply a vestige of "bourgeois formalism." This attitude reflects the habit of mind for which knowledge and truth have become ends in themselves. According to this outlook, the great virtue is "frankness" ("open covenants openly arrived at"). When frankness takes precedence, then tact and discrimination are branded "irrational." Modern man has no frame of reference in which to understand that he may be "factually right but morally wrong."[5] He can neither account for nor deal with the considerations upon which manners rest, which happen also to be the same considerations which Christianity takes most seriously: respect for personal dignity; the interplay of complex motives; and the consequent fact that the same word or deed might be quite appropriate in one situation and highly out of place in another. Each situation is different precisely because it involves unique emotional and volitional relations which, in turn, instead of being dismissed as "subjective" and irrelevant, are of decisive import.

Like any "rules of the game," manners serve a twofold function, the one protective, the other positive. Without rules, no holds are barred. Without manners, if human sin is a fact, then my neighbor is at the mercy of my own aggressiveness and disrespect. Especially when tempers are short and nerves are frayed, manners insulate against the sparks of animus which can so easily set off an explosion. They help prevent the kind of outburst which strains human relations past the breaking point.

Besides this negative function, rules provide the positive framework within which to exercise creative imagination in every situation. Without them, as satirists so often observe, the best of intentions become a bungling good will which often defeats its own aim. By structuring these amorphous sentiments, manners help to translate

[5]This pointed phrase, which contains the germ of an entire biblical theology, is used by Canon Edward N. West in his *Meditations on the Gospel of St. John* (New York: Harper & Brothers, 1955), p. 176.

them into concrete fact. Manners are important for Christianity precisely because it knows what the road to hell is paved with.

Like any good works, they are subject to abuse. They may become the vehicle of hypocrisy, where outward act is performed with intent to deceive. Christianity's remedy is not to abolish manners but rather to transform the motive. One of the reasons for the early growth of Christianity was that it possessed the resources for doing precisely this.

Again, when misunderstood, manners can also degenerate into "the letter that killeth," to the stultification of human relations. And again the answer does not lie in their abolition. Actually any such attempt is impossible. It only makes unruliness into a rule.[6] Moreover, the effect upon human relations is quite as lethal as the dead hand of formalism. By renouncing any principle of discrimination it robs man of his birthright as "discriminating animal" par excellence. Without such a principle nothing that a man says or does makes any appreciable difference. Life has gone stale. On the contrary, when manners are properly understood and applied, every word and every gesture acquire significance. They align themselves with either the creative or the destructive possibilities inherent in every situation. Christianity no more recognizes a separation between manners and morals than between morality and religion.

CONCLUSION

The biblical alternative is thus able to satisfy not only Augustine but Pelagius too. Its conception of joint responsibility is both truer to fact and far more serious than Pelagian individualism. By remembering that the good is not law but love it is free to appropriate the works of the law for its own creative purposes. He who does them from motives of self-salvation or the accumulation of merit is chasing after wind, for works alone cannot generate the only true goodness, love. The recognition that neither act nor theory alone can guarantee purity of motive is an additional strength of the biblical view. For, as has been shown above, the root error of the Augustinian and Reformation position is to try to prevent undesirable motives by means of a doctrine.

The biblical rationale for doing good works is simply that they can be well-pleasing to God and neighbor, and this in itself is the best of

---

[6]This point is made by Simone de Beauvoir in *The Ethics of Ambiguity*, translated by Bernard Frechtman (New York: Philosophical Library, 1948), p. 55.

reasons for doing them. Moreover, though they cannot create *agape*, they can create a milieu favorable to it. The primacy of love banishes the fear that one might be cheating if he tried to prepare for *agape* instead of just waiting for it to "happen." He who shrinks from "works" for fear of an impure motive cuts off his nose to spite his face.

There is no doubt, as Augustine and the Reformers saw, that good works *can* become the archenemy of love. But the same thing can happen to them that happened to another of Christianity's most zealous persecutors—St. Paul. Love will settle for nothing less than this: to transform its worst antagonist into an even more redoubtable ally.

CHAPTER XII

THE WORSHIP OF REASON

He taketh the wise in their own craftiness.
—Job 5:13

Christianity has sometimes displayed a genius for supporting the right position with the wrong reasons. It thereby does a
disservice both to itself and to the truth which it defends, for people
will assume that its affirmations are as faulty as the reasons it gives
in their support. An outstanding example is its attitude toward the
behavior and morals of non-Christians. Regrettable though these may
be, the appropriate reaction is not simply to pronounce judgment
and hurl anathemas. A far more responsible and painstaking procedure is called for, one which is based upon the distinctively Christian analysis of human nature. As was established in Chapter IV, the
proper definition of man is "religious animal," "homo religiosus," a
view which rests squarely upon an analysis of human freedom and all
that it entails.

In every act of choice there is at least a tacit reference to some
standard of value external to oneself. This source from which a man
takes his values, whatever it may be, functions as his "god." In this
functional sense of the word no free agent is without his "god." The
particular set of values with which it furnishes him governs his
specific decisions and in this way determines the quality of his entire
life. He has no choice between atheism and theism but only a
choice between gods. And every god stamps his worshiper with his
own trade-mark. The crucial question for every human life therefore
is: Which is the *true* god? Not until this question has been settled
can one designate the other "gods" as idols and their worship as sin.

It is therefore futile to object to pagan or "secular" values on the
grounds that they are sinful. They are only sinful *if* the gods which
sponsor them are false. The appropriate Christian reaction is therefore not indiscriminate denunciation but a careful examination of
the claims of these gods and an exposé of their shortcomings.

With characteristic wisdom the Bible's primary criticism of pagan
nations is that they "know not the Lord." If they did, they would
behave differently, or would at least acknowledge a criterion by which
their conduct could be judged. Until they do, it is futile to rail

against them. With the children of Israel, on the contrary, to whom the Lord has made himself known, it is entirely otherwise. They do have the "right" criterion but fail to live up to it. They acknowledge a frame of reference within which "our sins testify against us" (Isaiah 59:12). The ultimate sin for those who have known the true God is of course apostasy. To transfer allegiance from Yahweh to Baal is both the worst offense and the source of all other transgressions. No language is too strong for the prophets in their campaign against a "faithless generation" gone "whoring after false gods." But they reserve it for those who know better.

At the present time many theologians are keenly aware of the Church's tendency to forget the wisdom of the prophets and instead to belabor with moral strictures a generation which stands outside a Christian frame of reference and for which the word "sin" is consequently meaningless. The tendency today is to recognize that "sin" is relative to the "God" a man worships. We are rediscovering where the issue really lies. Men's value judgments, though supremely important, cannot be debated on their own merits. They are derivative from men's ultimate allegiance. Life is recognized today, as it has not been for several hundred years, as a battle of the gods.

THE DUPLICITY OF ALL FALSE GODS

At one point, however, contemporary thinking has not yet caught up with the Bible. Having traced men's values to their origin in ultimate commitment, it is diffident about adducing any criterion for distinguishing false gods from the true one (see Appendix). Here again the prophets were wiser than we. They knew that the truth must have some reason to commend it. Aware that the individual's value judgments are relative to his god, and therefore not directly debatable, they never doubted that the true God would vindicate himself. The classic picture of this prophetic confidence is Elijah's charge to an apostate people: "If Yahweh be God, then follow him; but if Baal, then follow him." He then proposes a very concrete test by which the false gods are exposed as frauds. This is the basic prophetic method of dealing with idols: to show that they cannot deliver on their promises. They entice their worshipers with glittering prospects and then visit them with cruel disillusionment. As Elijah taunts the priests of Baal: "Cry aloud; for he is a god: either he is musing, or he is gone aside, or he is on a journey, or peradventure he sleepeth and must be awaked." (1 Kings 18:27.) Because of the prophet's confidence in what the true God can do, he welcomes a test by which his impersonators can be unmasked.

An idol is a mountebank par excellence. The devil really is the father of lies. The worshiper of a false god is always foredoomed to betrayal. The story of Eve's temptation is a perfect illustration. When she allowed herself to be persuaded that her true interest lay in trusting the serpent's word instead of God's, she brought about her own undoing.

And when the woman saw that the tree was good for food, and that it was a delight to the eyes, and that the tree was to be desired to make one wise [all false promises implanted by the serpent], she took the fruit thereof, and did eat. (Genesis 3:6.)

Pagan philosophers and poets have stumbled upon this tendency of men to make unto themselves false gods and thereby destroy themselves. Before they can fit it into the pagan thought-world, however, they must first transpose it into something entirely different. By the time it has been digested by their impersonal categories it comes out as the famous "tragic view of life," according to which all human greatness necessarily runs amuck. Whether due to the jealousy of the god, as in some Greek drama (the original "tragedy"), or to a built-in metaphysical necessity, as in a philosopher like Schopenhauer, human frustration is held to be an ultimate law of life. Devotion to the good involves a man in hideous evil (like Creon in *Antigone*); the highest wisdom inflicts its possessor with blindness (Oedipus); exceptional natural ability brings upon a man his own destruction (Ajax).

It is understandable that nations who "know not the Lord" should regularly arrive at the "tragic view of life." Within their own frame of reference it is about as close as they could come to an awareness that idolatry, rather than an inscrutable Fate, is responsible for human catastrophe. For the Bible, on the contrary, only devotion to the *wrong* "good" results in evil; only wisdom directed to *mistaken* ends turns into blindness; only natural ability in the service of *false* gods issues in destruction.

Failure to distinguish clearly between the biblical and tragic views as mutually exclusive alternatives can lead to all manner of confusion and mischief. The following lines are a perfect illustration:

There is a . . . tragic law which controls the historical process, the law which ordains that human greatness utterly fall. There is human greatness in history . . . there are creative spirits and even some which have the power of knowledge and understanding. But just in being great and powerful and righteous they touch the divine sphere, and they become arrogant, and they are brought to nothing. They are without roots; they wither; the divine storm blows over them, and they vanish. That is the subject of Greek tragedy. *That is the message of the prophet to the nations of the world.* They are all subject to the law of tragic self-destruction. . . .[1]

The difference between the tragic and the biblical view, which the foregoing passage obscures, can be quite clearly stated. For the former the downfall of human greatness is automatic; for the latter it is due to misplaced allegiance. In the technical sense of the word it is not at all "tragic" because not necessary. In the more popular sense of the word it is all the more "tragic" for being avoidable. The real pathos of human life is that it *can* be so great, while men continue to make it so miserable, for themselves and for each other.

The professional pessimist sees one half the picture, the professional optimist the other. The former calls the latter superficial and is in turn pronounced defeatist. Each possesses a distorted fragment of the Christian truth. The Bible's realism exceeds that of the worst cynic, for it knows what man has done to God. At the same time its hope surpasses the wildest utopian fantasy, for it has concrete experience of what this same God will do for man.

An entire book could be devoted to this subject without exhausting it. For present purposes it suffices to expose the inner dynamics of idolatry by means of one full-dress example and then to cite more briefly in the following chapter additional illustrations of the same pattern.

THE RECORD OF THE GOD OF REASON

No idol, in ancient times or modern, has had a more consistent appeal than Human Reason. Lest this be misconstrued as an assault upon reason, let the chief characteristic of idolatry be emphasized once more. It always visits its victims with the opposite of what they expect. A critique of the idolatry of Reason is therefore undertaken, not in disparagement of intellect, but in its defense. The present

---

[1] Paul Tillich, *The Shaking of the Foundations* (New York: Charles Scribner's Sons, 1948), pp. 19f. My italics. The distinction between a Christian and a tragic view of life is persuasively drawn by Reinhold Niebuhr in his *Beyond Tragedy* (New York: Charles Scribner's Sons, 1938).

analysis will therefore argue that, when Reason is deified, its worshipers are led into blind irrationalism. If this can be demonstrated, the obvious implication is that the goal of complete reasonableness can only be achieved in a context of allegiance to the true God. Men may then take seriously the prophetic warning:

They that fashion a graven image are all of them vanity . . . Who hath fashioned a god, or molten an image, that it profiteth for nothing? . . . He falleth down unto it, and worshippeth, and prayeth unto it, and saith, Deliver me, for thou art my god . . . They have no knowledge that carry the wood of their graven image, and pray unto a god that cannot save . . . He feedeth on ashes. A deceived heart hath turned him aside, that he cannot deliver his soul, nor say, Is there not a lie in my right hand? (Isaiah 44:9,10,17; 45:20,21; 44:20).

Preliminary to examining the signs of our own times, it may be instructive to glance at four other epochs in history when Reason was exalted to divine status. Consider, for example, the very birthplace of rational knowledge, the source from which the founders of modern rationalism took their motto: classical Greece. And, of all Greece, consider its most enlightened city, Athens, home of Socrates, Plato, and Aristotle. And, of Athenian history, consider the Golden Age of Pericles and the years immediately following his death. Of this period a contemporary scholar has recently written:

The next thirty-odd years witnessed a series of heresy trials which is unique in Athenian history. The victims included most of the leaders of progressive thought at Athens—Anaxagoras, Diagoras, Socrates, almost certainly Protagoras, also, and possibly Euripides. . . . All these were famous people. How many obscurer persons may have suffered for their opinions we do not know. But the evidence we have is more than enough to prove that the Great Age of Greek enlightenment was also, like our own time, an Age of Persecution—banishment of scholars, blinkering of thought, and even . . . burning of books.

This distressed and puzzled nineteenth century professors, who had not our advantage of familiarity with this kind of behavior. It puzzled them the more because it happened at Athens, the "school of Hellas," the "headquarters of philosophy," and, so far as our information goes, nowhere else.[2]

Or turn to the chapter of modern history known as the Age of Reason. The fountainhead of this century of enlightenment was France and its culmination a movement designed to put into prac-

[2]P. R. Dodds, *The Greeks and the Irrational* (Los Angeles: University of California Press, 1951), pp. 189f.

tice the ideals of the great French philosophers—the same movement which unleashed an outbreak of hysteria and barbarism which shocked the civilized world, a Reign of Terror in which reason was swallowed up by passion. We miss the point of this unflattering episode if we forget that it was carried out in the name of Reason. No sooner had Roman Catholicism been banished from the churches throughout France than a new religion was officially installed in the same buildings. Known explicitly as the religion of Reason, it encouraged such rites as the famous incident in the Cathedral of Notre Dame, in which an actress from the opera, costumed as the goddess of Reason, received the homage of her worshipers. Statues of the saints gave way to busts of philosophers; the priest was replaced by the sage. History has preserved a sample of the kind of invocation addressed to this new deity:

Divine Reason. . . . thou who governest the destiny of men and empires, pray accept the homage which we come to render unto thee today . . .[3]

There was also a Revolutionary catechism, with a new version of the creed: "I believe in a Supreme Being, who created men free and equal, to love, and not to hate, each other, who prefers to be honored by virtue and not by fanaticism, in whose eyes the most pleasing form of worship is the religion of Reason and Truth . . ."[4] It is worth noting that this testament of sweet reasonableness concludes with a declaration of loyalty to the new republic and a ringing oath of destruction to all its opponents.

Consider a third example. In the first forty years of the twentieth century one single nation enjoyed the acknowledged intellectual leadership of the world. Its language was indispensable to anyone specializing in the sciences, philosophy, or scholarly pursuits generally. Yet in the space of five years this same language had made itself despised in most of Europe as the language of brutes and tyrants who had perverted their brilliant intellectual achievements to the irrational, diabolic service of "blood and soil."

And finally, although today's most obvious threat to rational endeavor is world Communism, it is sobering to recall that the Communists pride themselves on being the most scientific nation on earth. Karl Marx claimed to have stripped off all remnants of "bourgeois sentiment" and to have set up at last a "realistic" philosophy based

[3]Cited by A. Aulard, *Le Culte de la Raison* (Paris: Felix Alcan, 1904), pp. 104f.
[4]Ibid., p. 110.

upon the hard, cold facts of science and technology. And yet their blind devotion to this idol has led the present generation of Communists into absurdities and monstrosities without parallel in history. In the unforgettable lines of a former Communist:

The necessary lie, the necessary slander; the necessary intimidation of the masses to preserve them from shortsighted errors; the necessary liquidation of oppositional groups and hostile classes; the necessary sacrifice of a whole generation in the interest of the next—it may all sound monstrous, and yet it was so easy to accept while rolling along the single track of faith.[5]

The record is clear. When reason is exalted to divine status, it generates the seeds of its own destruction. What hidden logic is responsible for this? The answer is not far to seek. If we have not yet found it, this is because we are sitting on it. We suffer from the blindness which the idolator must always induce in himself before he can really put his trust in so transparent a counterfeit.

SOPHISTICATED NONSENSE

In our day the form taken by the worship of Reason is the deification of Science. The present purpose is simply to show that the Bible is being vindicated before our eyes. To that extent, it is definitely on the side of science and against its own suicidal tendencies. In the following paragraphs the scientist will be allowed to speak for himself. It goes without saying that the discussion concerns issues and not personalities and that by no means all scientists deify their method, nor do those cited do so consistently. Christians have so frequently made the mistake of attacking science itself, instead of its deification, that it is necessary to make this distinction quite clear. Science as an instrument in the service of man can be one of the greatest blessings on earth. It becomes an idol, however, the moment one says, with Bertrand Russell, "What science cannot discover, mankind cannot know."[6] The deception which underlies all idolatry can be detected beneath the surface of this statement. For there is no scientific means whatever of establishing its truth! It is therefore quite evidently in contradiction with itself. If one is going to enunciate an article of faith, one might at least make it consistent. But one of the hallmarks of idolatry is the falsehood on which it rests. As

[5]Arthur Koestler in *The God That Failed*, edited by Richard Crossman (New York: Harper & Brothers, 1949), p. 61.
[6]Bertrand Russell, op. cit., p. 238.

Isaiah so vividly puts it, "He feedeth on ashes. A deceived heart hath turned him aside that he cannot . . . say, 'There is a *lie* in my right hand.' " (Isaiah 44:20.)

If the biblical analysis is correct, then the result of such self-deception will be the opposite of what the devotee intends. In the present case it will turn out to be extremely unscientific. The hidden self-contradiction in Russell's statement leads one to anticipate precisely such an ironic outcome. It authorizes a method to dictate in advance the kind of question a man may raise and the limits to which his answers must conform. Indeed, reality itself, as far as man may know it, has been tailor-made to fit the advanced specification of a preconceived method. This amounts to the patently unscientific practice of torturing the facts to fit the theory.

The deification of science in our time is frankly stated by several of its devotees. One of them asks: "It comes down, then, to this: shall we put our faith in science or in something else?"[7] He answers his rhetorical question thus:

In our time and for some centuries to come, for better or for worse, the sciences, physical and social, will be to an increasing degree the accepted point of reference with respect to which the validity (Truth) of all knowledge is gauged.[8]

The same confession of faith is made even more explicit by another contemporary writer:

Men bet their lives on it (science) as they do on other gods, and on the record, it functions no less divinely than any other believed to shape human ends. On the record, "God" is no less fitting an appellation for this . . . than for any that churchmen so name and require laymen to bet their lives on, worship, and adjure.[9]

This faith reduces itself to faith in a method. Its practical implications are readily apparent. As one of its adherents declares, the scientific dogma includes the refusal even to entertain any question which the sacred method cannot answer: "The motive is to find an answer that meets the requirements of a scientific answer."[10] Here is science

[7]George A. Lundberg, op. cit., p. 114.

[8]Ibid., p. 36.

[9]Horace M. Kallen, *Democracy's True Religion* (Boston: The Beacon Press, 1951), p. 10. Although the context is not clear, it is possible that the author is referring here to science in partnership with democracy.

[10]G. A. Lundberg, op. cit., p. 19. See also Max Otto, *Science and the Moral Life* (New York: The New American Library, 1949), p. 155.

become a religion. The same enterprise which can render unlimited service to man by examining the subject matter to which its method corresponds slips into the role of tyrannical false god the moment the individual scientist *decides* that no other subject matter may be legitimately investigated. All the great issues of human life, all the questions that make it interesting and worth while, are suppressed. They all require qualitative judgments; in the last analysis, judgment of good and evil. But the scientific method is able to cope only with quantitative subject matter, with what can be measured. The truth has a long last laugh at the expense of this idolatry. For the refusal to make qualitative judgments, including judgments of value, turns out to be fatal to the entire rational enterprise. Without some qualitative principle of selection the scientist is unable to distinguish the important data from the unimportant. All facts are in themselves of equal value. It would be "partial" to rank some higher than others. The determination to maintain "scientific neutrality" leads to the preoccupation with trivial detail and thus partly justifies the layman's common-sense suspicion of academic activities. Although the scientist himself may be unaware of the absurdities into which his "impartiality" betrays him, it is painfully evident to the Chinese author, Lin Yutang, who writes:

It is easy to see why the Chinese mind cannot develop a scientific method; for the scientific method . . . and inductive reasoning, carried over to human relationships, . . . often results in a form of stupidity not so rare in American universities. There are today doctoral dissertations in the inductive method which would make Bacon turn in his grave. No Chinese could possibly be stupid enough to write a dissertation on ice cream, and after a series of careful observations, announce the staggering conclusion that 'the primary function of sugar (in the manufacture of ice cream) is to sweeten it'; or after a methodical study in 'Time and Motion Comparison on Four Methods of Dishwashing', happily perceive that 'stooping and lifting' are fatiguing; or that, in 'a Study of the Bacterial Content of Cotton Undershirts', 'the number of bacteria tends to increase with the length of time garments are worn.' . . .

This sort of stupidity . . . could really be arrived at, I think, just as correctly by a moment of Chinese common sense and 'intuition'. The best cartoon I have ever seen in *Punch* is that of a congress of behaviorists, who after passing a number of pig-'subjects' through a test, with a thermometer in the snout and a pearl necklace dangling in front, unanimously resolve that pigs do not respond to the sight of jewelry.[11]

[11]Lin Yutang, *My Country and My People* (New York: A John Day Book, Reynal & Hitchcock, 1935), pp. 86f The author documents his quotations from the *Teacher's College Record* (Columbia University, February 1930), p. 472.

These observations ought to silence the favorite reply of contemporary devotees of Reason. When confronted by the repeated fiascoes into which this idol has historically beguiled its worshipers, they argue that a sufficient effort has never yet been made. The noble pioneers of Reason were defeated in times past by the lingering forces of ignorance, superstition, and vested interest. To desert them at this hour would be a "failure of nerve." We must rally round Reason to insure that this time it will triumph at last and so vindicate its martyrs of the past. As Lin Yutang's remarks clearly demonstrate, the irrationalities of an Age of Reason are due, not simply to a residue of "prescientific thought-ways," but to a direct consequence of the dictatorship of science itself. It has remained for the twentieth century to contrive a brand of nonsense to which less "advanced" cultures are happily immune.

MAN THE VICTIM

Unfortunately, when the consequences of idolizing science are applied to the big questions of human nature and destiny, something terrible happens to man's understanding of himself. His freedom is repudiated, since science could never discover it; his judgments of good and evil are reduced to expressions of appetite, since this is measurable; and human motivation is transformed into a complex set of conditioned reflexes. Two quotations from contemporary scientists illustrate this perfectly: "To a scientist, the motives of a stone rolling down hill or of a boy murdering his father are simply the full set of circumstances resulting in either event. These conditions are equally subject to scientific investigation in both cases."[12] The man of science consequently strives to be as ethically neutral as possible:

There is perhaps no better introduction to the meaning of science in our time than the study of the scientific attitude of Francis Bacon. . . . He was a scientist in the whole temper of his mind. . . . He was a far truer scientist than some whose laboratory genius has won them recognition as great scientists in the twentieth century, yet who quickly return to unscientific obscurantism when faced with ethical or religious problems. That he was almost utterly lacking in ethical dependability has often been pointed out. He did not hesitate to demean himself, to prosecute his talents, or to betray his friends, if this promised to secure him advancement. . . .

[12]G. A. Lundberg, op. cit., p. 19.

It is very doubtful if a more unemotional human being ever existed than Francis Bacon. He was as nearly pure brain as it is possible for a man to be. . . . Kuno Fischer has accurately characterized him: 'If there were a thermometer to measure intrinsic force of human passions, we should find, in the case of Bacon, that the degree of warmth belonging to his heart stood very close to zero.'

This lack of emotional warmth, which was responsible for his most flagrant defects of character and for that conspicuous trait which David Hume described as his 'extraordinary facility in helping himself,' *also made him the more perfect intellectual machine.* It fitted him the better to take part in what he called the 'disinterested observation of nature.' He exemplified in his own person the ethical neutrality of science; the recoil of science from every consideration of the wished-for or the ought-to-be; the concentration of science upon the study of what is, has been, or is bound to come. He was, as it were, science itself.[13]

This description beautifully illustrates what happens when man tries to deny his own nature. He is that creature who, because he is free, *must* make value judgments. His only choice is the choice between values. He cannot remain "neutral." Whereas Christianity regards this characteristic of man as the precondition of his highest fulfillment, most other philosophies are ashamed of it, as an obstacle to "scientific objectivity," and try to suppress or transcend it. If the Christian contention is true, however, then the attempts to suppress value judgments will backfire. He who worships at the shrine of "neutrality" will in fact become unscrupulous. An imagined objectivity, adopted in the name of impartial reason, provides the excuse for unprincipled conduct. Remarking upon exactly the same phenomenon in the age of Greek rationalism, Professor E. R. Dodds remarks:

The new rationalism did not *enable* men to behave like beasts—men have always been able to do that. But it enabled them to justify their brutality to themselves, and that at a time when the external temptations to brutal conduct were particularly strong. As someone has said in reference to our own enlightened age, seldom have so many babies been poured out with so little bath-water.[14]

Of course, such an outcome is far from the intentions of today's men of science. This is precisely what gives the situation "its irony and its urgency." They would die if their right hand knew what their left hand was doing. In some parts of the world scientists already have died because it did not.

With the bath of bigotry and superstition goes the baby of ethical

[13]Max Otto, op. cit., pp. 77f. My italics.
[14]E. R. Dodds, op. cit., pp. 191f.

awareness. Having arrived at scientific maturity, we have outgrown
the primitive need to make judgments of good and evil. This constitutes an open invitation to unbridled lawlessness and particularly to
the tyranny of man over man. To put it in a formula, relativism is
the prelude to absolutism. The twentieth century is noteworthy for
both these "-isms" at once. On the one hand, speaking with the
authority of science, it declares the relativity of all moral judgments.
On the other, it has seen the moral vacuum filled by the mushroom
growth of political absolutism surpassing anything in previous history.
The major contributor to relativism was science. The principal victim of the ensuing absolutism is, likewise, science. What happens to
science in totalitarian countries needs no elaboration. The result of
laboratory experiments are dictated in advance by party theory. The
scientist who cannot arrive at doctrinally correct results is punished.

As an alternative to such a fate, the devotee of science may advocate
instead his own version of totalitarianism. He recognizes no moral
scruple against it and, in fact, is impatient with the irrationality and
inefficiency of the masses. Hence he may be tempted to write of the
"technically obsolete paraphernalia" of traditional democratic proc-
esses and to declare:

The mere fact that I, personally, happen to like the democratic way of
life with all its absurdities . . . and that I may even find it worth-while
to go to any lengths in defense of democracy of the type to which I am
accustomed are matters of little or no importance as touching the scientific
question at issue. My attachment to democracy may be, in fact, of scientific significance chiefly as indicating my unfitness to live in a changing
world. To accept this simple notion is perhaps a cost of social science
that few are willing to pay. . . .
A similar attitude toward the conclusions of social scientists is sus-
pected of being authoritarian, as indeed it probably is. A lot of nonsense
has been spoken and written about authority in recent years. We need
to recognize that it is not authority as such that we need fear but in-
competent and unwisely constituted authority. . . .[15]

If what men really need is to be ruled by "competent" authority, it
is obvious who the twentieth-century successor to medieval authority is. The scientist steps forward as the modern version of Plato's
philosopher-king.

Unlike Caesar, some scientists apparently are not at all diffident
about accepting such a role. Professor B. F. Skinner, in his recent
book *Walden Two*, outlined with a completely straight face his con-

[15] G. A. Lundberg, op. cit., pp. 39, 46, 51f.

ception of the ideal society. It is an autocracy in which such a power
is exercised by a scientist able to control precisely all the thoughts
and actions of its citizens. As Joseph Wood Krutch said of man's lot
in this ignoble utopia:

His desires, tastes, convictions and ideals are precisely what the experi-
menter wants to make them. He is the repository of no potentialities
which can ever develop except as they are called forth by circumstances
over which he has no control. Finally, of course, his happy condition is
the result of the fortunate accident which determines that the "engineer"
who created him and, indirectly, will create all his progeny, was an ex-
perimenter whose random conditioning happened to produce, not the
monster who might just as likely have been the first to seize the power
that science offered, but a genuinely benevolent dictator instead.[16]

It was just such a nightmare as this against which Aldous Huxley
sought to warn the world twenty years ago in his satire *Brave New
World*. Mr. Krutch observes ironically that it is as though Professor
Skinner had read *Brave New World* without seeing the point.

Perhaps the most distressing tribute which the idol of science
exacts from its devotee is the sacrifice of his rightful human heritage
as a free, evaluating individual, for whom to live is to exercise his
discriminating and critical faculties. The man who carries this graven
image from the laboratory to the hearth resolutely sets out to remake
his every reflex into the image of his god. He becomes undiscriminat-
ing, literal-minded, matter-of-fact, lacking in subtlety or humor—in
short, insufferably dull. One such victim remarked, after the curtain
had fallen on *Hamlet*, "Why does he say, 'I am dead, Horatio,' when
he is obviously still alive?" This is the lost generation of whom the
president of the Carnegie Foundation has said:

Higher learning has fallen for the 'cult of objectivity, (which) has resulted in a generation of irresponsible intellectuals, of men without convictions' . . . The average history textbook, for instance, 'which so often
determines the tone of classroom instruction, is chiefly a recital of fact
. . . objective, non-controversial, a record of events. It recounts what
happened . . . but often fails to ask why it happened (or) what the
meaning is . . .
'The implication is that education which takes a detached view of life
and society, that never leads students to face issues . . . tends to produce
men and women who are spectators rather than actors. . . . Surely the
effective citizen must be willing to stand up and be counted, to make a
commitment, to throw his weight on the side of truth . . .
'Pursuit of the truth is undoubtedly the highest function of the uni-

[16]J. W. Krutch, op. cit., p. 62.

versity, but that is not synonymous with scientific research. It refers to search for reality, for meaning, for ultimate answers . . . Commitment to certain basic assumptions is a necessary starting point in the quest for truth. . . .'[17]

FALSE GOD, FALSE PROMISE

The deification of science is thus exposed as self-defeating on three different levels. In the very bastion of rationality, the American university, it has a tendency to magnify the trivial, the tedious, and the inconsequential. On the level of society as a whole it lends itself to the kind of totalitarianism whose first aim would be the prostitution of science. On the personal level, most horribly of all, it helps to rob man of his birthright. By foisting off upon him the machine as his ideal to imitate, it converts him into a puppet ready to dance to the dictator's command. By means of an unconscious propaganda, it instills into modern man the fatal belief that he is, in fact, no more than a bundle of conditioned reflexes. The consequence of this belief is a complete contempt for the very rational process which postulates it. Joseph Wood Krutch has captured in the space of several sentences the suicidal effect of this kind of rationalism:

One might almost as well give up the whole enterprise of thinking if one never permits oneself to say, "I am convinced of so and so," without adding immediately, "But of course I recognize that it is either certain or at least highly probable that I would not be convinced of anything of the sort had it not happened that my social or individual conditioning had made it inevitable that I should be."

Yet it is actually some such *radical distrust of all human reason* that is encouraged by the pronouncement sometimes made by men who may not really wish to produce any such effect and may not actually hold deterministic theories in their most extreme form.[18]

The victim of this triple self-defeat exhibits the telltale symptom of all idolatry. He remains unperturbed when these suicidal tendencies are pointed out to him. Having once committed himself to his god, he is loath to acknowledge the glaring discrepancy between its promises and its performance. Rather than grant that his loyalty has been misplaced, he prefers the grim satisfaction of knowing that he has done his "duty"—even where this "duty" requires him to walk the plank. Hence the astonishing reaction of some scientists when

---

[17]Dr. Oliver C. Carmichael, as quoted in *Time* magazine, December 1, 1952, p. 47.
[18]J. W. Krutch, op. cit., p. 203. My italics.

the inevitable result of their own "theology" is pointed out to them. They declare with a fatalistic smile that no mere human sentiment must be allowed to impede the requirements of Science. Thus does enlightened twentieth-century man unwittingly repeat the primitive follies which he imagines himself to have outgrown. He is willing to lacerate himself, even to immolate his whole society, in the appeasement of a totem of his own concoction.

Despite its modern dress, this is no new god. It claimed a sizable share of victims in biblical times. Their epitaph was written by St. Paul: "Professing themselves to be wise, they became fools" (Romans 1:22.) The biblical message to our men of science might run something like this: "You have launched a gigantic undertaking in search of rationality and knowledge. May your enterprise prosper, and may the Lord bless it. But remember that, in the moment in which you make it an end in itself, it will trick you into sophisticated stupidity." The handwriting is on the wall. It requires no Daniel to read it.

APPENDIX

There are three reasons why contemporary theologians are reluctant to argue for the superiority of their own God. The first is the fear of presumption, lest "finite man" claim to know what is supremely true. This is another example of "ideology of conscience," which abandons the question of true-or-false in the hope of finding an intellectual formulation which will guarantee the virtue of whoever utters it. Whenever truth is trifled with in this way, it gets revenge. Whoever makes use of an argument in order to insure his own virtue is saying, in effect, "Holier than thou," to anyone who challenges it. He is thus delivered into the very fault which he set out to avoid.

There is a second reason why some contemporary theologians hesitate to adduce reasonable grounds for declaring the Christian God to be the true one. They fear lest any reason in God's favor would both subject him to an alien criterion and also constitute an "ulterior motive" for believing in him. This contention, like so many other emphases in contemporary theology, is unconsciously borrowed from the mystical tradition. It is descended directly from the maxim of St. John of the Cross: "A blind man, if he be not totally blind, will not commit himself wholly to his guide."[19] Rational argument is thus

[19]Cited by P. E. More, op. cit., pp. 59f.

actually regarded as an impediment to pure faith. Theologians who would prefer to believe *without* reason, rather than with it, are consequently at pains to prove that the Christian God is utterly irrational, accessible only by a "leap of faith." They thereby give their case away. They have an undeclared argument of their own. The irrationality in which they take such satisfaction is just as much an "ulterior motive" as any reasonable argument.

There is a third and final reason why contemporary theologians are reluctant to discriminate between gods. It is the fear of religious fanaticism. If a man can prove that his God is the true one, they argue, he will feel justified in imposing his belief upon others. This, however, is only an argument of expediency, and, like all such arguments, it turns out to be inexpedient. For, if no ultimate allegiance has any reasonable claim to superiority, then "the master race" or "the party" is quite as acceptable as any other god. There is no reasonable ground upon which to oppose them. The argument thus turns out to be self-defeating. It must either acquiesce in the conquests of a Hitler, and thereby in its own liquidation, or, if it does oppose him, it must do so for no good reason. In which case it has committed suicide. For the active suppression of a given set of values, simply because they are "not mine," was the very mistake which the argument set out to avoid. Christianity has the answer to this problem. Although it claims to know *the* truth, this truth itself includes a prohibition against conformity by compulsion. Whenever Christian practice violates this injunction, it stands condemned by its own principles.

CHAPTER XIII

GRAVEN IMAGES IN MODERN DRESS

> They that fashion a graven image are all of them vanity; and the things that they delight in shall not profit.
>
> —Isaiah 44:9

In its examination of the worship of reason the previous chapter developed the inner dynamics which involve all idolatry in self-defeat. The present chapter will apply this principle to a number of other contenders for the hearts of men. Of all contemporary false gods, none is more seductive than that which goes by the name of "idealism." Its advocates can be so persuasive. "Now that God has been made obsolete by modern knowledge," they argue, "why not salvage Christianity's abiding gift to the world, its lofty ideals, by dissociating them from the baggage of ancient superstition?" In other words, we cannot really be sure whether there is a God or what he is like. But we can be sure about ideals. How much more realistic, therefore, to base one's religion on them.

This proposal has been so widely accepted that in many people's minds the words "idealistic" and "religious" have become synonymous. Yet it does not differ essentially from the one which confronted the prophets. It is simply a modern variation on the old, old theme, "Let us transfer our faith from God and put it in something else." The following pages will show how this most plausible kind of idolatry is subject to the same fate as the worship of Reason. When made absolute, ideals, too, visit the worshiper with the opposite of what he had expected.

TWO ELUSIVE VIRTUES

To begin with an illustration familiar to everyone, the virtues of humility and unselfishness provide a perfect example. No one can consciously cultivate humility for its own sake without at the same time becoming *proud* of it. The same is true of unselfishness. Like true humility, it is a by-product of something else—of love. The real problem is not, how can I be humble or unselfish? but, how can I love my neighbor as myself? When the attempt is made to bypass the real problem, to construct a facsimile of real love by imitating some of its external coloring, then these two ideals turn into their contraries. Self-conscious humility becomes the source of pride, and cultivated unselfishness becomes a subtle instrument for dominating others. No one has discovered more convincing evidence of this than the psychiatrist. As Erich Fromm expresses it:

The "unselfish" person "does not want anything for himself"; he "lives only for others," is proud that he does not consider himself important. He is puzzled to find that in spite of his unselfishness he is unhappy, and that his relationships to those closest to him are unsatisfactory. . . . Analytic work shows that . . . he is pervaded by hostility against life and that behind the façade of unselfishness a subtle but not less intense self-centeredness is hidden. . . .

The nature of unselfishness becomes particularly apparent in its effect on others and most frequently, in our culture, in the effect the "unselfish" mother has on her children. She believes that by her unselfishness her children will experience what it means to be loved and to learn, in turn, what it means to love. The effect of her unselfishness, however, does not at all correspond to her expectations. The children do not show the happiness of persons who are convinced they are loved; they are anxious, tense, afraid of the mother's disapproval, and anxious to live up to her expectations. Usually, they are affected by their mother's hidden hostility against life, which they sense rather than recognize, and eventually become imbued with it themselves. Altogether, the effect of the "unselfish" mother is not too different from that of the selfish one; indeed, it is often worse because the mother's unselfishness prevents the children from criticizing her. They are put under the obligation not to disappoint her; they are taught, under the mask of virtue, dislike for life.[1]

TOLERANCE

Another example is the ideal of tolerance. Tolerance is certainly a desirable virtue, but it can only be made absolute on the assumption that no conviction is any more true or false than any other. And this assumption itself quickly leads to the end of tolerance. The challenge of a Hitler confronts its followers with an impossible dilemma. Either, in loyalty to their god, they stand petrified while Hitler unmasks it, or else they must forsake their idol and become intolerant of intolerance. Their embarrassment becomes acute when they are asked *why* they resist Hitler. Since for them all convictions are relative, why is his any less valid than theirs? On their own principles they can only fight him because they do not happen to like him. The reason why they do not like him is his utter lack of principle. In

[1] Erich Fromm, op. cit., pp. 132f.

opposing him without any principle of their own, therefore, they do the very thing which they abhor. Their idol has betrayed them into precisely the sin from which it promised deliverance.

The twentieth century is noteworthy for two things. First, it is the century of relativism. The mark of the enlightened man is the axiom that all standards of truth and goodness are relative to the individual or to his culture. The idolatrous nature of this formula becomes especially apparent whenever it is promulgated, not on its merits at all, but in order to provide a rationale for tolerance. In plain words this amounts to the subordination of the question of true-or-false to an ulterior motive. Even though the motive is the lofty one of tolerance, it has nevertheless been made into an idol. The result is exactly what the prophet would predict; namely, the second characteristic of our age, absolutism. Relativism always invites absolutism. Since no man can be without some standard of truth and goodness, then the denial of any objective criterion simply constitutes the first step toward the declaration, "*My* good is *the* good." By what argument can such a claim be refuted? By none, if all standards are relative. Thus does tolerance, both in theory and in fact, sign its own death warrant.

HUMANISM

Another favorite is humanism. Man himself is elevated to the top of the cosmic ladder. The deification of man has pervaded nearly every aspect of recent culture. In the philosophy of Auguste Comte the God of Christianity is explicitly replaced by Humanity. The same conviction is expressed by Swinburne's lines, "Glory to Man in the highest! for man is the master of things."[2]

This deification of man, however, is mocked by the grim facts of contemporary life. This is the century of the degradation of man. The theme of so much current, agonized poetry, for example, is precisely the dehumanization of our age. T. S. Eliot's *The Wasteland* and W. H. Auden's *The Unknown Citizen* have become classic laments at the transformation of the glorious vision of Renaissance man into the pathetic spectacle of bewildered and apologetic John Doe. The apotheosis of man in theory has resulted in his degradation in fact. What is this but a repetition of the ancient story? Man has again fallen for the serpent's stratagem: "Ye shall be as gods." In

[2] Cited by Reinhold Niebuhr, op. cit., Vol. 1, p. 3.

trying to take over the role of God he has brought only humiliation upon himself.

The crown with which modern man proclaimed himself king was science. But this crown has turned into a hangman's noose. For science regards man as it would any other animal. It converts the children of God into test-tube fodder. This process has reached the point where our novelists imagine that they are derelict in their duty if they fail to depict human life as morbid and despicable. It has become "unrealistic" and "escapist" to suggest that it can be meaningful or ennobled or joyous. In the words of Nicolas Berdyaev:

> The image of man has been shaken and has begun to disintegrate after it was revealed. This is going on now in all spheres. Dehumanization has penetrated into all phases of human creativity. In making himself God man has unmanned himself. . . . The new world which is taking form is moved by other values than the value of man or of human personality, or the value of truth: it is moved by such values as power, technic, race-purity, nationality, the state, the class, the collective.[3]

Such is the bitter surprise which the idol of humanism has in store for its worshipers.

COMMUNISM

This discrepancy between humanism's theory about man and his actual plight in the modern world partly explains the magnetic appeal of one of the most virulent of all idolatries: Communism. This man-eating monster is not always recognized as an idealism. Yet the tremendous personal sacrifices it exacts from its disciples are demanded in the name of the brotherhood of man and prosperity for all. It has attracted so many sensitive idealists precisely because it promises to translate the impotent oratory of liberal humanism into concrete fact. The words of the "Internationale" struck such a responsive chord among men who yearned for a world of fraternity and equality that some are still unable to recognize their sickening contradiction by the facts of Soviet life.

The way in which conversion to Communism corresponds, point by point, to the biblical analysis of idolatry has been beautifully illustrated by a book with the appropriate title, *The God That Failed.*[4]

[3]Nicolas Berdyaev, *The Fate of Man in the Modern World*, translated by Donald A. Lowrie (New York: Morehouse Publishing Company, 1935), p. 22.

[4]Richard Crossman (ed.), *The God That Failed* (New York: Harper & Brothers, 1949).

It is a soul-searching analysis by six former Communists and Communist sympathizers of the way in which the devotee falls prey, body, mind, and soul, to this false god. His scruples are silenced by its very idealism; his eyes are blinded by its clever lies; and finally, if he ever does wake up to these continual betrayals, he either escapes with his life or becomes a sacrificial victim.

At first glance it is difficult to realize that Communism really is idealistic in its appeal rather than a cynical design for world dominion. Seen from the inside, however, it still *claims* to be on the side of equal justice for all, especially the oppressed and exploited. As Louis Fischer eloquently recalls:

> The Bolsheviks glorified the common man and offered him land, bread, peace, a job, a house, security, education, health, art, and happiness. They championed international brotherhood. . . . They proudly liberated Poland, Finland and the Baltic countries from Russia's rule. They renounced the Czar's special privileges in China and his spheres of influence —with its oil concession—in Persia. The oppressed of the world, and the friends of the oppressed, accordingly saw Soviet Russia as the herald of a new era.
> . . . A thrill shot through humanity.[5]

It was the very nobility of the Communist ideal that induced sensitive souls to give it their unreserved allegiance. In terms of the biblical understanding of human freedom this commitment was "religious" through and through. Arthur Koestler confirms this in the following words:

> New light seems to pour from all directions across the skull. The whole universe falls into pattern like the stray pieces of a jigsaw puzzle assembled by magic at one stroke. There is now an answer to every question, doubt and conflict are a matter of the tortured past—a past already remote, when one had lived in dismal ignorance in the tasteless, colorless world of those who *don't know*. Nothing henceforth can disturb the convert's inner peace and serenity—except the occasional fear of losing faith again, losing thereby what alone makes life worth living, and falling back into the outer darkness where there is wailing and gnashing of teeth.[6]

Richard Wright makes exactly the same testimony: "With the exception of the Church and its myths and legends, there was no agency in the world so capable of making men feel the earth and the people upon it as the Communist Party."[7] Whereas the two preceding state-

---

[5]See Richard Crossman, op. cit., p. 199.
[6]Ibid., p. 23.
[7]Ibid., p. 155.

ments are reflections by the disillusioned, they are perfectly corroborated by lines from the diary of André Gide, written in the days when he still believed in Communism:

My conversion is like a faith. My whole being is bent towards one single goal, all my thoughts—even involuntary—lead me back to it. In the deplorable state of distress of the modern world, the plan of the Soviet Union seems to me to point to salvation. . . . And if my life were necessary to assure the success of the Soviet Union, I would gladly give it immediately. I write this with a cool and calm head, in full sincerity, through great need to leave at least this testimony, in case death should intervene before I have time to express myself better.[8]

Having allowed Communism to become the keeper of his conscience, the convert can easily be persuaded, out of loyalty to his new faith, to suppress his own sense of right and wrong. Of all the disclosures in the book, none is more poignant than the vivid account of how men of sincerity and good will permit themselves to be blinded. In Arthur Koestler's eloquent words:

There is always a supply of new labels on the Cominform's black market in *ideals*.

Every single one of us knows of at least one friend who perished in the Arctic subcontinent of forced labor camps, was shot as a spy or vanished without trace. How our voices boomed with righteous indignation, denouncing flaws in the procedure of justice in our comfortable democracies; and how silent we were, when our comrades, without trial or conviction, were liquidated in the Socialist sixth of the earth. Each of us carries a skeleton in the cupboard of his conscience; added together they would form galleries of bones more labyrinthine than the Paris catacombs.[9]

The main burden of the book is its account of the process by which the six authors awoke from their gruesome nightmare. In every case the awakening occurred as a result of the eventual realization, despite their own efforts to shut their eyes and stop their ears, that this god was a fake. Under the banner of lofty ideals, and undoubtedly courageous deeds, it had enticed millions of unsuspecting persons of good will to their death—physical, spiritual, or both. Louis Fischer traces his own disillusionment to the gradual and belated discovery: "In place of idealism, cynical safety-first. In place of dedication, pursuit of personal aggrandizement. In place of living spirit, dead conformism, bureaucratic formalism, and the parroting of false clichés."[10]

[8]Ibid., p. 173.
[9]Ibid., pp. 71, 74. My italics.
[10]Ibid., p. 217.

One is tempted to formulate the rule: The loftier the ideal which one deifies, the ghastlier the ultimate outcome.

DEMOCRACY AND NATIONALISM

But Communism is by no means the only political god that will fail. There is another closer to home, one which in itself is certainly the finest instrument thus far devised for giving political implementation to Christian principles: democracy itself. Because the Church has often failed to see this, and because powerful Christian spokesmen have in time past unfortunately sought to obstruct its growth, the present discussion will undoubtedly be labeled an attack upon democracy.[11] In fact, of course, it is the exact opposite. The question is merely raised whether democracy, as one of man's greatest blessings, will turn into its opposite if made an end in itself. If there is strong evidence that it will, then the present discussion is in democracy's interest. This will not prevent hysterical cries that this book is anti-democratic, but it will at least establish that they are hysterical.

Although Americans have not yet succumbed to the temptation to deify democracy, this kind of irrational reaction is an alarming symptom. Instead of discussing the issue on its merits, some writers immediately resort to the Communist technique of impugning the motives of anyone who raises the question. In a recent pamphlet entitled "Democracy and Clericalism," for example, one author declares that anyone who argues that "morality can exist only on a dogmatic theological basis" is seeking to use the prevailing tensions in our country to serve his own ends. Charges like this are a sure symptom of idolatry. The relation, if any, of morality to theology is one which can and should be settled on its merits. To charge one side in the argument with ulterior motives is a convenient way of evading the issue. The same author brands discussions like the present one as an attack upon "those who defend democratic ideals as enemies who seek to establish democracy as a rival religion. These are vague, meaningless statements but they are dangerous because they exploit primitive fears and confuse the average person into thinking that he is against religion to the extent that he believes in democracy as a moral

[11] For an accurate account by a convinced Christian of the predominantly negative attitude of Christianity toward democracy in the past, see James H. Nichols, *Democracy and the Churches* (Philadelphia: The Westminster Press, 1951).

way of life."[12] The substitution of epithet for argument is a sign of idolatry at work.

One does not have to look far to uncover the inner logic by which the idolization of democracy entails its doom. Democracy is really only a procedure for the controlled expression of the will of the people. When this mere procedure is made ultimate, when there is no higher criterion of truth and goodness, the result is the sanctification of the popular will. Truth is reduced to a matter of majority consensus, ascertainable by public-opinion polls. If the majority is always right, then dissent is automatically wrong. This view has already found a foothold among us. A committee of Congress recently advised the tax-free philanthropic foundations to be "chary of promoting ideas, concepts, and opinions forming material which runs counter to what the public currently wishes, approves, and likes."[13] Such advice provides a rather miserable contrast with the aims and convictions of our founding fathers. Nevertheless, it was recently given the halo of scientific authority by a social psychologist when he said:

Adjustment means a state of mental health, which condition becomes synonymous with the American concept of living . . . to adjust means to accept the existing values and to accept that which is viewed as unalterable reality. Adjustment therefore means blending into the group without showing any signs of deviation.[14]

Does this have a familiar ring? Where else is "deviationism" the cardinal sin? Fortunately not all social scientists have succumbed to this idol. Dr. Robert Lindner recently denounced "the rot-producing idea that the salvation of the individual, and so of society, depends upon conformity and adjustment."[15] If America ever does adopt the view that the majority is always right, then, in the name of democracy, we will have stifled individual freedom in a strait jacket of conformity. We may still call it "democracy," but it will no more deserve the name than the so-called "people's democracies" of eastern Europe.

One of Communism's most transparent hypocrisies is its use of the slogan of world brotherhood to disguise its imperialistic ambitions. It

[12]Agnes E. Meyer, "Democracy and Clericalism." The Ware Lecture, published by The American Unitarian Association, Boston, 1954.
[13]As reported in the New York *Times,* January 7, 1955, p. 12.
[14]Jurgen Reusch and Gregory Bateson, *Communication* (New York: W. W. Norton & Co., 1951), p. 129.
[15]Reported in *Time* magazine, December 6, 1954, p. 65.

thus works hand in glove with another idol, one which the prophets had continually to oppose: the perennial god of nationalism. This idol has an especially strong attraction, as Reinhold Niebuhr has pointed out, for two reasons. On the one hand, it is enough bigger than the individual to give him a sense of disinterested self-sacrifice, even though it may in fact be merely the servant of collective egotism. On the other hand, it is sufficiently concrete and intimate to evoke a strong emotional response. Hence no false god offers a more constant temptation than nationalism, personified, as it often is, by Caesar or Führer. And hence the unerring insight of the prophet into both the nature of this idolatry and its futility:

Say unto the prince of Tyre, Thus saith the Lord God. Because thine heart is lifted up and thou hast said I am a God, I sit in the seat of God, in the midst of the seas. Yet thou art a man, and not God, though thou set thine heart as the heart of God. By thy great wisdom and by thy traffic hast thou increased thy riches, and thine heart is lifted up because of thy riches. Therefore thus saith the Lord God: Because thou hast set thine heart as the heart of God, behold, therefore I will bring strangers upon thee, the terrible of the nations. And they shall draw their swords against the beauty of thy wisdom, and shall defile thy brightness. They shall bring thee down to the pit, and thou shalt die the deaths of them that are slain in the midst of the seas. Wilt thou yet say before him that slayeth thee, I am God? But thou shalt be a man, and no God, in the hand of him that slayeth thee. (Ezekiel 28:2,5,6-9.)

It is not only Communism which plays into the hands of a national god. Democracy, too, when made an idol, can serve the same purpose. When the mere process of democracy is made ultimate, then there is no higher criterion by which the results and direction of the process may be judged. Anything a given nation does is then automatically justified, provided only that it is a democracy. This means that to differ with such a nation over matters of policy is to be wrong by definition—not merely incorrect, but morally derelict; that is, undemocratic. What complicates present American relations with India, for example, is the fact that, although Prime Minister Nehru is undoubtedly mistaken in his estimate of Communism, some United States spokesmen, by impugning his motives, make it impossible for him to discover his error. This only drives a potential ally further in a direction which would ultimately be disastrous for both countries.

The surest sign of nationalistic idolatry is the identification of truth with a given nation's mood of the moment. As Hitler put it, "Whatever serves the German people is right." The consequence of this is the equation of honest difference with malevolent or treasonable intent. To describe the present paragraph as antidemocratic or anti-American, for example, would simply provide an exquisite illustration of this point. Heaven forbid that Ignazio Silone's observation of the Communists should ever apply to America:

What struck me most about the Russian Communists, even in such really exceptional personalities as Lenin and Trotsky, was their utter incapacity to be fair in discussing opinions that conflicted with their own. The adversary, simply for daring to contradict, at once became a traitor, an opportunist, a hireling. An *adversary in good faith* is inconceivable to the Russian Communists.[16]

A very simple test will determine whether our own country ever falls into such an ominous condition. Do we say that a thing is American because it is good, or *vice versa?* The former case implies a standard transcending national limits by which a particular thing may be judged good and therefore incorporated into American life. In the latter case, whatever happens to be American is "good" by definition. This would be idolatry wearing the mask of patriotism. There was a day when a patriot could write, "America, America, God mend thine every flaw." We will know that that day is over when this hymn is censored on the ground that it asks God to engage in un-American activities. It would then be too late for warning. Instead, the ancient prophecy will come true once again:

How much she [Babylon; read "any idolized nation"] hath glorified herself and lived deliciously, so much torment and sorrow give her. For she saith in her heart, I sit a queen, and am no widow, and shall see no sorrow. Therefore shall her plagues come in one day, death, and mourning, and famine; and she shall be utterly burned with fire: for strong is the Lord God who judgeth her. (Revelation 18:7,8.)

Communism, being idolatrous in its very nature, will inevitably fan the fires of nationalism. Democracy, on the contrary, since it is only a method, albeit a precious one, need not become an end in itself. On the contrary, it can become a chosen instrument in the service of the true good and thereby not only save itself but brighten the hopes of mankind as well. In these momentous times the course of history for hundreds of years to come hinges upon whether "this nation, under God, shall have a new birth of freedom—that government of the people, for the people, by the people, shall not perish from the earth."

[16]See Richard Crossman, op. cit., p. 101. My italics.

THE GOOD THAT I WOULD

The inner necessity by which a deified ideal betrays its worshiper provides the clue to the famous and much misunderstood exclamation of St. Paul: "The good that I would, I do not. And the evil which I would not, that I do." (Romans 7:19.) This has frequently been construed as an expression of the view that sin is intrinsic to human nature. It is then paraphrased as: "The conditions of human existence are so impossible that no matter how clearly I see and desire the good, any attempt to translate it into action necessarily corrupts it." Such an interpretation fits naturally into the "tragic view of life," according to which any supposedly "good" action entails an equivalent amount of evil, so that the "good that I would" automatically turns before my eyes into the "evil which I would not."

As it stands, St. Paul's statement is susceptible to this interpretation, but it is equally amenable to another, very different construction, one consistent with the whole context of biblical thinking. On this interpretation it is simply a perfect description of the result of making an idol of any ideal. It is a classic expression of the bewilderment of the idolater on discovering that his best intentions have been perverted by the false god for purposes he never intended.

CHAPTER XIV

THE HIDDEN GODS OF CYNICISM

The fool hath said in his heart, There is no God.
—Psalm 14:1

According to the Bible, life confronts every man and nation with a decisive either/or: choose the true God, and live; or choose a false god, and perish. There remains one final device by which men have sought to escape this choice. It is cynicism, the attempt to avoid entanglement with the fickle gods of idealism by espousing none at all. It generally takes the form of a frank policy of selfishness and expedience. When this alternative is refuted, the last link in the biblical argument will have been completed.

If the biblical analysis is correct, a thoroughgoing self-centeredness is impossible. Man *cannot* make himself the sole center of his own life. His freedom necessarily relates him to something beyond himself. The proper diagram of even the most selfish life is therefore not a closed circle but an ellipse with two centers, representing the false god around which the individual makes his orbit. Theologians have not always expressed this as clearly as a contemporary lay author, who writes:

There is even in the most selfish passion a large element of self-abnegation. It is startling to realize that what we call extreme self-seeking is actually self-renunciation. The miser, health addict, glory chaser and their like are not far behind the selfless in the exercise of self-sacrifice. Every extreme attitude is a flight from the self.[1]

If this were more widely recognized, Christianity would not make the mistake of championing "selflessness" as the highest good. It could only be so if self-centeredness were the worst evil. But since self-centeredness is not even possible for a free agent, the Christian conception of good is not the meaningless goal of "selflessness" but the abandonment of every false god for the true one.

An examination of cynicism reveals exactly what the biblical analysis would lead one to expect. Every cynic turns out to be a covert idealist, in the sense that he does gravitate toward some standard outside himself as the criterion of his decision. Moreover, no matter

[1]Eric Hoffer, *The Passionate State of Mind* (New York: Harper and Brothers, 1955), as reported in *Time* magazine, March 14, 1955, p. 114.

how different his particular standard is from those of other men, the cynic cannot consistently speak or think of it without calling it "good." In his heart of hearts he really believes that although not commonly recognized as such, or perhaps precisely *because* of this, it is a "better" good than the conventional standards of the average man. In fact, the real motive power behind his apparent lawlessness is generally some hidden virtue. Most often it is the virtue of honesty. Perceiving the hypocrisy of the idealist, he fancies his own disillusioned outlook to be truer to the facts of life. The Communist's self-righteous contempt for "bourgeois idealism" is a familiar illustration. The zeal behind his fanatical denunciations is derived from the hypnotic power of his own "higher" ideal. His counterpart in the history of philosophy is Friedrich Nietzsche. He named his heartless hero after Zoroaster because he stood for "the truth" against the deceit and pretension of the moralist. Another of the cynic's secret virtues may be kindness. Perceiving the vindictiveness with which the pharisee feeds upon the shortcomings of others, he often professes contempt for all morality whatever. Despite his effort at concealment, this kind of cynic turns out to be a sheep in wolf's clothing. In the moment of crisis it may be he who puts into practice what the moralist is content to preach. Of the countless literary expressions of this theme none surpasses the example of Sydney Carton.

The refutation of the cynic thus requires two steps: the exposure of both his hidden ideal and of the self-deceit in which it involves him.

THE REBEL

Perhaps the hardiest garden variety of cynicism is the glorification of rebellion and iconoclasm for their own sake. Man's true greatness, it claims, lies in the consistent defiance of whatever law or custom happens to prevail at the moment. In continental Europe this adolescent psychology has been developed into a full-fledged philosophy, propounded in the last century by men like Michael Bakunin and in our own by Albert Camus in his recent book, *The Rebel*.

The hidden ideal which pulls the strings of this sophisticated vandalism is not far to seek. It is the liberty and integrity of the individual. It is beneath the dignity of man, so runs the argument, to submit to any externally imposed pattern. Bakunin, for example, for all his revolutionary nihilism, was at the same time a transparent idealist. The destruction which he demanded was a prelude to the flowering of a "more perfect" society of liberty and equality.

Whenever an idol persuades its worshiper to advocate rebellion for its own sake, his betrayal is accomplished. He becomes the victim of an upside-down legalism. The rebel's bondage to the law of nonconformity is quite as real as the legalist's subservience to established norms. The pride with which he negates every "finite" attainment is quite as offensive as the moralist's self-righteousness. Having undertaken rebellion as the only way of preserving his freedom, he becomes thereby a manacled member of the wrecking crew.

SEX

A second familiar form of cynicism is the unprincipled pursuit of sex for its own sake. In Germany, where it has achieved official literary endorsement, the obsession with sex is called the cultivation of *"das ewige Weibliches,"* the "eternal feminine principle." It is personified by the legendary figure, Don Juan. In his tone poem of this name Richard Strauss quite frankly describes his ambition as the mortification of individuals in the name of the species.[2]

Yet the cult of sex is not so cynical as it sounds. Although it does mortify individuals, it does so in the service of a supposedly "loftier" ideal: the "eternal." In the words of a recent best seller, woman is a groined archway into the infinite. The word "infinite," of course, gives the case away. It is part of the standard terminology of idealist religion. Owing precisely to its sublime, "spiritual" connotation, it proves in operation one of the most mischievous of fictions. It overrides any "merely finite" considerations. For who has the right to resist the hypnotic call of "the Infinite" (uttered in a wide-eyed stage whisper)? The famous mystery religions of Graeco-Roman times were dedicated to this seductive ideal. In many of their cultic rituals a conspicuous role was played by sex.

History abounds with proof that the worship of this god is self-defeating. The French moving picture *La Ronde* is simply an aesthetic meditation on this subject. Contrary to what the hue and cry about censorship would lead the public to believe, it is a poignant exposé of the futility of the pursuit of sex for its own sake. The New York *Times*

[2] See Frederick Niecks, *Program Music in the Last Four Centuries* (London: Novello and Company, Ltd., 1906), p. 499.

critic Bosley Crowther discerned the real point of the film when he
wrote:

"La Ronde" is emphatic about one thing: that is the bleak futility of any
substantial satisfaction from an adventure in illicit love. . . . For those
who would seek excitement in wanton and clandestine amours, pleasure
is flimsy and fleeting . . . the mental build-up of expectation is pure
illusion and nothing more.[3]

The purport of the picture is nevertheless not the Christian but
the tragic view of life. Its theme is that everyone is "destined" to be
continually duped by the anticipated satisfaction of an experience
which regularly turns to ashes in the moment of its achievement. Life
is a merry-go-round of successive disenchantments. Its only compensa-
tion is the disillusioned smile of those who at least know that they
are the victims of a mocking fate. When laughter is at one's own expense, far more prudent to join in than to be the unwitting butt of a
bad joke.

Perennial testimony by high priests of the religion of sex bears out
the Christian analysis. The Byrons and Stendhals frankly confess to a
diminishing capacity for sensual enjoyment. In the end many of them
admit a fundamental antipathy to women. Some are so frank as to
grant that their primary satisfaction lay, not in the consummation of
their conquest, but in the subtleties of deception and seduction which
preceded. The psychology of this kind of idolatry receives penetrating
literary treatment in Sören Kierkegaard's *Diary of the Seducer*.[4] It is
described in the following terms by a contemporary psychotherapist:

It is an axiom in psychiatry that a plurality of direct sexual outlets in-
dicates the opposite of what it is popularly assumed to indicate. Dividing
the sexual interest into several objectives diminishes the total sexual
gratification, and men whose need for love drives them to the risks and
efforts necessary to maintain sexual relations with more than one woman
show a deficiency rather than an excess in their masculine capacities. . . .
Don Juanism is another familiar pattern in which the seducing, disappointing, and abandoning of women leaves no doubt of the hostility felt
for them. Promiscuity is a symptom, whether in men or in women, of
an essential inability to find deep satisfaction anywhere. Such persons do
not love their sexual objects; they seek rather to conquer them or to
destroy them. What is often described in such moralistic terms as selfishness or caddishness or faithlessness is from a pychological standpoint un-
explained by such terms. It is rather a relative "malelessness." Such men

[3]See the New York *Times*, March 21, 1954, section 2, p. 1.
[4]Sören Kierkegaard, *Either/Or*, Vol. I, translated by D. F. Swenson and Lilian M.
Swenson (Princeton University Press, 1946).

are constantly trying to prove to themselves and sometimes to others that they are as masculine as their inner voices tell them they are not.[5]

A Christian would raise the further possibility, as Kierkegaard does, that Don Juan's impotence may be quite as much the result of his obsession as the cause. Thus is another of the greatest gifts of God to man destroyed when made ultimate.

MONEY

Another form of cynicism, one requiring no illustration in our day, is the glorification of money. Although at first glance many people do seem to cherish it for its own sake, it is never really an end in itself. Money is power, and power in any form is sought only for what it can *do*. If a man were doomed to permanent exile on a desert island, he would waste no love on money. It is only a means to some other end, such as prestige, or security, or "gracious living."

None of these things is bad in itself. But, when made the central focus of a man's whole existence, they exhibit the same duplicity as any other false god. Their favorite stratagem is to encourage the illusion that they can be bought. Once persuaded of this, the worshiper busily invests financial transactions with the solemnity of a religious ritual. As a contemporary social analyst comments:

Money is officially coined *mana*. Whether they realize it or not, its users are participating in a religious observance. Whoever observes a modern bank with its Doric columns and high marble halls, whoever notices the ceremonious demeanor of teller and patron, can scarcely avoid the feeling that a cultic ritual is being performed.[6]

The disillusionments of this kind of idolatry are only too well known. The worshiper may have intended his devotion to money to be only temporary, a provisional means to a worthier end. By the time he is ready to begin enjoying his wealth the modern Midas discovers too late that the things he really wants are not for sale. First, the kind of prestige money will buy can never compensate for the gnawing discontent with which he regards himself. This explains the pathetic act of self-humiliation in which the totalitarian dictator gives himself away. Notwithstanding his unlimited power over men, he

[5]Karl Menninger, *Love Against Hate* (New York: Harcourt Brace and Co., 1942), pp. 59, 72f.
[6]Th. Bovet, *Die Angst vor dem Lebendigen Gott* (Bern: Verlag Paul Haupt, 1948), p. 34. My translation.

stoops to the level of bribing school children to compose lyrics of
love and gratitude to their benevolent protector. Second, the kind of
security which money provides is precisely the kind which moth and
rust corrupt, which thieves can break in and steal. The rich, not the
poor, are the principal victims of robbery and kidnaping. Finally, in
a luxuriously appointed residence the "gracious living" which the
idolater seeks may be all the more conspicuous by its absence. Its
prime prerequisites are positive, joyous human relations. Without
these, attractive furnishings only cry out for somebody who knows
how to use and enjoy them. This accounts for the perplexed dismay
of the prosperous citizen who has dutifully taken orders and accepted
promises from the almighty dollar. The secret of gracious living has
been withheld from him and vouchsafed to less comfortable homes.
Thus hath God chosen the weak things of the world to confound
the things which are mighty (1 Cor. 1:27).

DESPAIR

Finally, it remains to discuss one of the most predatory of current
idolatries, the cult of despair. It has gained a foothold in nearly every
facet of contemporary life, whether literature, painting, politics,
philosophy, or even theology. It is symbolized by the title of Jean
Paul Sartre's novel *Nausea*; intellectualized by the "abyss of nothingness" which existentialist philosophers conjure up by a clever exploitation of emotional language; and summarized in the following
terms by George Grosz. Explaining one of his own works, the picture
of a painter confronting a canvas with a large hole in it, he says: "This
painter once believed in something, but now he paints only a hole,
without meaning, without anything—nothing but nothingness, the
nothingness of our time."[7]

Like other expressions of cynicism, the cult of despair gains
plausibility by appealing to two ideals, honesty and courage. This
twofold appeal is illustrated by the following passage from a contemporary author:

Existentialism, that is the great art, literature, and philosophy of the
twentieth century, reveal [*sic*] the courage to face things as they are and
to express the anxiety of meaninglessness. It is creative courage which
appears in the creative expressions of despair. . . . Modern art is not

[7]Reported in *Time* magazine, January 25, 1954, p. 90.

propaganda but revelation. It shows that the reality of our existence is as it is.[8]

Adherents of this cult become convinced of their unflinching honesty by implying that no meaning in life can be detected without rose-colored glasses. Only the pessimist is the true realist. They persuade themselves of their superior courage by hinting that their opponents lack the nerve to face up to the grim facts.

This, like nearly every error, is parasitic upon the truth. The grain of truth which it distorts is the fact that if God, his words and his acts, are subtracted from reality, the remainder is quite as bleak, and the plight of man quite as desperate, as the existentialist contends. This is precisely what one would expect. A God who was worthy of the name could not be ignored with impunity. The issue is one of fact: can he be disregarded consistently with the principles of intelligent inquiry, or not? Instead of examining the question on its merits, the existentialist will not tolerate the slightest suggestion that life may be meaningful.

This must be one of the devil's favorite idolatries. At least its self-defeat is accomplished with singular dispatch. The claim of honesty is refuted by the despair-monger's reaction to counterargument. Instead of troubling to refute it he employs a short cut. He simply implies that it is a cowardly (or "bourgeois" or "superficial") device for evading the grim truth. Whenever questions of true-or-false are resolved by resort to epithet, the claim of honesty is forfeit. If there were a meaning in life, the existentialist would never be able to discover it. He has prejudged the case with his own peculiar version of "ideology of conscience."

What ulterior motive prevents him from inquiring honestly into the question? The answer is not far to seek. His claim to courage would collapse if life were meaningful. In order to make the claim plausible, he must picture himself as in a constant state of anguish at the gruesome character of existence, yet bravely refusing to hide it from himself by any comforting myth. His game has been perfectly analyzed and succinctly expressed by Macaulay in his essay on Byron:

Year after year, and month after month, he [Byron] continued to repeat that to be wretched is the destiny of all; that to be eminently wretched is the destiny of the eminent . . . His principal heroes are men who have arrived by different roads at the same goal of despair, who are sick of

[8]Paul Tillich, *The Courage to Be* (Yale University Press, 1952), pp. 143, 147.

life, who are at war with society, who are supported in their anguish only
by an unconquerable pride resembling that of Prometheus on the rock;
whose heart had been withered, whose capacity for happiness was gone,
. . . but whose invincible spirit dared the worst that could befall . . .
here or hereafter.[9]

If reality is not so horrible as Byron pretends, then he at once
ceases to be a tragic figure and becomes comic. In actual fact he is
comic in any case. For he has never bothered to find out what reality
is like. His is an imaginary world, invented to fulfill his desire to play
the hero. He thereby betrays himself into the hand of the ironic
nemesis which awaits every idolater. For it is he who turns out to be
the wishful thinker! Beneath all the fine words about honesty and
courage he finds a perverse satisfaction in the "romantic agony." In
the writings of our modern Cassandras it is quite evident that they
could not bear to be deprived of their hothouse gloom. They revel
in the repulsive, vie with each other in conjuring up disgusting
imagery, and rejoice at the least indication of human frustration. If
they discover these things where the rest of the world does not, this
only convinces them of their superior sensitivity. Gerard Manley
Hopkins has perceived the hidden gratification behind this show of
martyrdom and coined the appropriate term for it: "carrion comfort."[10]

Earlier writers, less afflicted with the messianic complex, have
sometimes acknowledged despondency to be a form of self-indulgence.
Burton's *The Anatomy of Melancholy* contains an acute analysis of
this phenomenon. It was illustrated in the last century by the fashion
among romantic poets of composing odes to melancholy in the
spirit of Leigh Hunt's couplet:

> Mirth is deceit, and laughter folly,
> Bliss wafts the sigh of Melancholy.[11]

Admissions like this expose the claim to courage as an affectation.
The cultivation of despair is really a means of avoiding all risk. As
Helmut Kuhn has said of existentialism, it seeks to become immune
to crisis by embracing crisis. This is simply a sophisticated version of
the slang aphorism, "If you can't beat 'em, join 'em." The vaunted

[9]T. B. Macaulay, *Essays* (New York: D. Appleton and Co., 1860), p. 127.

[10]Gerard Manley Hopkins, "Carrion Comfort," in *Poems of Gerard Manley Hopkins* (New York: Oxford University Press, 1948), p. 106.

[11]Leigh Hunt, "Melancholy," in *The Poetical Works of Leigh Hunt*, edited by
H. S. Milford (Oxford University Press, 1923), p. 737.

courage of the ancient Stoics is subject to the same criticism. Their pessimistic outlook on life was deliberately contrived in order to insure against any possible disappointment. Epictetus admits this:

The good man can suffer no defeat. Of course, for he engages in no contest where he is not superior. . . . You can be invincible, if you never enter on a contest where victory is not in your power.[12]

Far from being courageous, such an attitude betrays an excessive preoccupation with one's own security. It is at bottom the fear of fear. The following comment by Harry and Bonaro Overstreet unmasks its pretension and reduces it to proper proportions:

What an individual feels impelled to say about himself is often, indeed, a good practical clue to his state of ill-being or well-being. Thus, when a nine- or ten-year-old boy boasts stridently, "I'm not scared of anybody or anything!" the perceptive adult knows the boy is scared. Otherwise his mind would not be on the subject of whether or not he was scared.[13]

Thus does the false god once again lead its worshiper into a trap. When courage is made absolute it drives its devotee to invent despair without regard to reality. It thereby catches him in the very wishful thinking he had set out to avoid.

AND GOD SAW THAT IT WAS GOOD

The foregoing analysis suggests the formula: scratch a cynic and you find an idealist. His more "realistic" goals are simply the bait with which some standard of goodness lures him. Like the acknowledged idealist, he too is rewarded with the opposite of what he wants. Enough has already been said to distinguish this process from the "tragic view of life." One further misunderstanding remains to be dispelled.

The present chapter might suggest that since money, sex, and the criticism of rigid moralism all serve to decoy men into futility, then they should resolutely be forsworn. This is the perennial doctrine of contempt for all worldly things. The Stoic Marcus Aurelius expresses it as follows:

The rottenness of the matter which is the foundation of everything! Water, dust, bones, filth: or again, marble rock, the callosities of the

---

[12]Epictetus, *Discourses*, Book III, Chapter 6; *The Manual of Epictetus*, Aphorism 19.
[13]H. and B. Overstreet, op. cit., p. 52.

earth; and gold and silver, the sediment; and garments, only bits of hair; and purple dye, blood; and everything else is of the same kind.[14]

Such a view is utterly irreconcilable with the biblical conception of the goodness of creation. All the good things of life were intended by God for man's use and enjoyment. Only when they become ends in themselves, or when they are put to the service of wrong ends, are they destructive. The Christian therefore emphatically does not renounce any material object, any temporal activity, simply on the ground that it is "worldly." For him "worldly" is a positive, not a pejorative, word. He renounces it only if he cannot use it constructively. And when this does happen it reflects on him, not upon the thing he gives up.

Not money, but the love of money, is the "root of all evil." Conversely, not poverty, but the right of use of money, is a great good. Christianity, as an all-or-nothing religion, is willing to wager that money will continue to be responsible for evil until it is subordinated to the love of God. The same is true of sex. It should not surprise the Christian if sex only made men happy when blessed by God. History certainly suggests that it otherwise makes them wretched. And, finally, the rebel's complaint against legalism might also be expected to miscarry when independently conducted. Without the Christian alternative it becomes sheer destructiveness. The *only* live alternative to legalism is *agape*. The whole point, of course, has been much more succinctly and eloquently expressed: "Seek ye first his kingdom, and his righteousness, and all these things shall be added unto you." (Matthew 6:33.)

[14]Marcus Aurelius, *Meditations*, IX, par. 36.

CHAPTER XV

HEARTS OF FLESH

Except ye repent, ye shall all likewise perish.
—Luke 13:3

If human freedom cannot be consistently denied, and if its exercise entails the distinction between good and evil, then no man is without some conception of sin. If both the moralistic view and the view of sin as intrinsic to human nature are fatal to freedom, then they must be discarded. Conversely, if the biblical understanding of sin as idolatry is rooted in an appreciation of freedom, and if all men do in fact orient their lives toward some god or other, then the central question of human existence is: Which of all the rival claimants is the true God? If the mark of a false god is the betrayal of its worshipers into bondage and hardheartedness, then the true God is One who could be counted upon to set them free by empowering them to love.

All this, of course, is pure theory. The most it can do is to induce a man to ask the right questions. Once he does, he is astonished to discover that they are precisely the questions to which the unsophisticated Bible has all along been speaking. Crediting him with enough wisdom to ask them, it dispenses with the preliminaries and speaks directly of a God who has historically made and kept his promises to men. There is consequently no better description of its message than the traditional understatement, "good news." It purports to record the events in which such a God "proclaimed liberty to the captives" by imparting to them the gift of *agape*.

There is, however, a prerequisite to becoming a beneficiary of these mighty acts: repentance. The mention of this word precipitates a debate with a discipline which thus far has provided scientific support for many stages of the argument: psychotherapy. It is worthwhile rehearsing the many ways in which the analyst's clinical data have been of inestimable value in the recovery of the biblical conception of human nature. They have confirmed, for example, that in certain areas a man's reason is the servant of his will and that the results of rational inquiry will vary with the orientation of the heart. Many analysts, notably the school of Harry Stack Sullivan, have reached the wholly biblical conclusion that one's mental and emotional health depends upon his human environment and that the absence of love induces neurosis. Psychiatry has also provided valuable ammunition for the refutation of the two pagan versions of sin. It has rendered obsolete the assumption, based upon a jaundiced view of human nature, that self-assertion per se is sinful and self-denial virtuous. It has shown that, on the contrary, pride and self-contempt, though logical opposites, are inseparable twins which mutually aggravate each other. As against moralism, psychiatrists have exposed the self-righteousness and hidden vindictiveness of the moral vigilante, as well as the destructive effects of any ethical rule when it becomes a superego. Finally, they detect the emotional hypocrisy by which the legalist hides his secret inclinations from himself and the world. Fritz Kunkel observes that Christendom has often tended to regard character difficulties as something to be shunned, never to be discussed or investigated. "Sin is bad, and the good man turns away in horror. This emotional attitude is one of the gross fallacies of theology."[1]

Most important for present purposes, the psychiatrist discovers more than enough evidence for hardness of heart, and all the concrete acts of hostility that go with it, to confirm the biblical doctrine of the universality of sin. According to one psychiatrist, those who have undergone the psychotherapeutic process recognize that weakness and inner torment are "the common property of all and that no one can point the finger of scorn at his fellow."[2] This substantiates St. Paul's declaration, "Wherein thou judgest another, thou condemnest thyself; for thou that judgest doeth the same things" (Romans 2:1).

Karl Menninger is more specific in his analysis of the subtlety with which sin disarms its victim by operating within the explicit "rules of the game," or even by masquerading as virtue:

More painful to the man are those innumerable attacks upon his masculinity which the frustrated wife inflicts in the course of the daily routine of life, the things that are discussed in every column of advice to the lovelorn—neglecting, reproaching, distrusting, criticizing, ridiculing, interfering with pet hobbies and habits, playing the martyr and giving the impression of being the victim of the husband's suspicion or cruelty, disappointing him in major or minor expectations, improvidence, tardiness, and so on. It seems invidious to make such a list, which must necessarily be not only incomplete but equally applicable to husbands.

[1] Fritz Kunkel, *In Search of Maturity* (New York: Charles Scribner's Sons, 1949), p. 34.
[2] Beatrice M. Hinkle, "An Introduction to Analytic Psychology," in *An Outline of Psychoanalysis*, J. S. Van Teslaar, ed. (New York: Modern Library, 1925), p. 252.

Aggression is not the monopoly of either sex. The object of aggression is to hurt, to make unhappy, to destroy; and all the techniques available to a woman who is unconsciously hostile toward her husband she will use against him.[3]

With unlimited evidence of this kind at his disposal, one would expect the psychiatrist to be receptive to the biblical categories of guilt and repentance. Yet this is precisely the point of his sharpest attack upon Judaism and Christianity. Feelings of guilt, he argues, are demonstrably the worst impediments to the healthy expression of the personality. By discovering their hidden causes, the analyst helps the patient to dispel them. One consulting psychologist declares, for example, that, consciously or otherwise, parents use their children as whipping boys,[4] and one of the commonest kinds of abuse is to burden them with a mountainous sense of guilt. When the victim finally realizes that his unfounded guilt feelings were originally planted by the contradictory demands of a domineering parent, they lose their strangle hold on his creative capacities. The therapist has seen so much similar mental suffering caused by fulminations and threats from the pulpit that the whole conception of sin is anathema to him. When he dispels such *misplaced* guilt, he undoubtedly functions as an angel of mercy.

Suppose, however, that there were a residue of genuine guilt, consisting of destructive attitudes and actions for which one were truly responsible. What could be done to remove it? One thing only: forgiveness. But this is not at the psychiatrist's disposal. The fact of real guilt, as opposed to misplaced guilt, would consequently confront him with a problem he could not solve within the limits of scientific techniques. Instead of inquiring disinterestedly whether in fact there be any such objective guilt, he often sets out to reduce it all to mere feelings which can be explained away. This entails the denial of human responsibility for evil and the consequent suspension of moral judgment. The self-contradictory nature of any such attempt, as analyzed in Chapter II, is illustrated in this instance by Karen Horney's perplexity over what to do with moral rules. Having declared that "should's," as she calls them, only serve to inhibit the natural flow of man's vital forces, she is confronted by the awkward implication that they *should* be abolished. The only way out of this diffi-

[3] Karl Menninger, *Love Against Hate* (New York: Harcourt, Brace and Co., 1942), pp. 116f.

[4] See Dorothy Baruch, *New Ways in Discipline* (New York: McGraw-Hill Book Company, Inc., 1949), p. 260.

culty is to decide on reconsideration that some "should's" are right
after all—a position which is undoubtedly true, but which she has
left herself no means of establishing.[5]

The attempt by some psychiatrists to suspend value judgments is
nicely illustrated by their substitute for forgiveness, the depressingly
neutral word "acceptance." To "accept" is what the scientist does
with laboratory data. He acknowledges the facts without evaluating
them. Acceptance does have a provisional place within a Christian
context, in so far as it stands against a censorious attitude toward
one's neighbor. "Judge not, that ye be not judged," for "vengeance is
mine, saith the Lord" (Matthew 7:1, Romans 12:19). It also stands
for facing facts squarely, including the facts of sin. Moreover, it can
serve as a reminder that *agape* requires love for the total person,
rather than for selected parts. If made ultimate, however, acceptance
reduces man to the level of a laboratory specimen, without freedom
or responsibility. It thereby provides another illustration of the
humanist's dilemma. Originally invoked by the humanitarian concern
to prevent cruel moral condemnation, its ultimate effect is the degradation of man. The humanist's determination not to point the guilty
finger results in a patronizing attitude which is quite as inhumane.
This is nicely illustrated by Erich Fromm's attempt to give meaning
to moral judgments after he has denied freedom:

In making value judgments one judges facts and does not feel one is godlike, superior, and entitled to condemn or forgive. A judgment that a
person is destructive, greedy, jealous, envious is not different from a
physician's statement about a dysfunction of the heart or the lungs. . . .
We can even assume that we would have become like him had we lived
under the same circumstances; but while such considerations prevent us
from assuming a godlike role, they do not prevent us from moral judgment. *The problem of understanding versus judging character is not
different from the understanding and judging of any other human performance.* If I have to judge the value of a pair of shoes or that of a
painting, . . . I may have sympathy or pity for the shoemaker or the
painter, . . . but I can not say that I can not judge his work because I
understand why it is so poor.[6]

Despite his humane intentions, the psychiatrist who puts character
on the same level as shoemaking is really addressing the moral delin-
quent in the same words which children use to hurt an unco-operative
playmate: "Leave him alone—he can't help it." Even granting, for the

[5] See Karen Horney, op. cit., pp. 364, 374, *et passim.*
[6] Erich Fromm, op. cit., pp. 236f. My italics.

sake of argument, that this could be done without an attitude of "holier than thou," it suggests a cool smugness which is quite as intolerable. The aloof condescension of the expert toward the "morally inferior" is hardly less godlike than the sanctimoniousness which he deplores. It assigns every man to a moral pigeonhole. To the extent that it denies him the dignity of freedom and responsibility, acceptance turns out to be a disguised form of rejection!

The alternative to this unintended belittling of man, and to the self-contradictions which it entails, is to grant the reality of freedom, responsibility, and guilt. Karl Menninger actually does this. "This guilt lifting," he says, "is an equivocal blessing. I, for one, think that some guilt feelings are better *not* removed—they belong."[7] To take this step is to acknowledge the urgency of repentance and forgiveness. A psychiatry which does this, far from replacing Christianity, makes it more relevant than ever. It raises questions and discovers problems which nothing besides Christianity and Judaism has ever claimed to answer—questions which require an answer beyond the limits of psychiatric techniques. The most immediate is, "How can we retain value judgments without fastening upon each other's conscience a paralyzing burden of guilt?" To put it differently, if we acknowledge human freedom, and with it the facts of responsibility and guilt, are we not obliged to cry, with the prophet, "Woe is me, for I am undone. For I am a man of unclean lips, and I dwell in the midst of a people of unclean lips"?

The question reflects the incredulity of men generally toward the good news of Christianity. If freedom exists, they reason, then guilt is a reality; far better to take away freedom than to admit the insoluble problem of unforgiven guilt. They cannot bring themselves to grant the possibility of a God who forgives, much less to allow him the opportunity to do it. This was foreseen by the ancient prophecy:

Behold, ye despisers, and wonder, and perish: for I work a work in your days, a work which ye shall in no wise believe, though a man declare it unto you (Acts 13:41).

The wisdom of the world reckons without a God who comes "not to condemn the world, but that the world through him might be saved" (John 3:17).

Christianity stands or falls with the claim that this God has acted

[7] Karl Menninger, "What the Girls Told," in *The Saturday Review*, October 26, 1953, p. 30.

within history to fulfill his promises: to forgive sins and incorporate men in a redemptive community, here and now. The indwelling presence of God enables the members of this community, despite their manifest imperfections, to bind up and renew *agape* as often as it is cast down and broken. Living in the midst of a brutal society, this Church, in the New Testament sense, can absorb and neutralize the world's malevolence. It grows by drawing the sting from the worst that men can inflict.

The redemption which the Church offers to all men is deliverance from bondage to the idols which have blinded and enslaved them. It liberates by conferring upon them the one thing which they can scarcely acquire by effort, *agape*. It thereby hastens the day when it will be fully what it already is in part: the fulfillment of God's ancient promise,

I will take away the stony heart out of your flesh, and I will give you a heart of flesh (Ezekiel 36:26).

This gift of a transformed heart frees men at last to come into their own; to inherit the high destiny originally prepared for them; to exult with a joyous company in the glorious liberty of the sons of God.

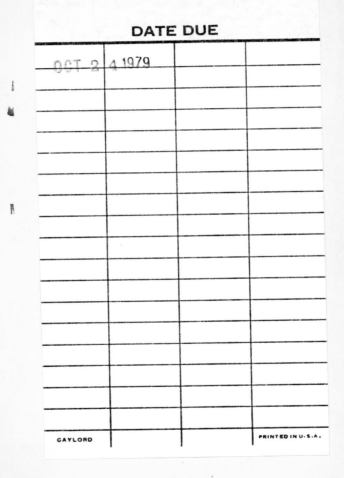

DATE DUE

OCT 2 4 1979			
GAYLORD			PRINTED IN U.S.A.